27 Kid-Pleasing Cover-ups for

est of **Fons&Porter**

fun QUILTS for kids

LEISURE ARTS
the art of everyday living
www.leisurearts.com

FONS & PORTER STAFF
Editors-in-Chief Marianne Fons and Liz Porter

Editor Jean Nolte
Assistant Editor Diane Tomlinson
Managing Editor Debra Finan
Technical Writer Kristine Peterson

Art Director Tony Jacobson

Editorial Assistant Mandy Couture
Sewing Specialist Cindy Hathaway

Contributing Photographers Dean Tanner, Katie Downey, Craig Anderson
Contributing Photo Assistant DeElda Wittmack

Publisher Kristi Loeffelholz
Advertising Manager Cristy Adamski
Retail Manager Sharon Hart
Web Site Manager Phillip Zacharias
Customer Service Manager Tiffiny Bond
Fons & Porter Staff Peggy Garner, Shelle Goodwin, Kimberly Romero, Laura Saner, Yvonne Smith, Anne Welker, Karla Wesselmann

New Track Media LLC
President and CEO Stephen J. Kent
Chief Financial Officer Mark F. Arnett
President, Book Publishing W. Budge Wallis
Vice President/Publishing Director Joel P. Toner
Vice President/Group Publisher Tina Battock
Vice President, Circulation Nicole McGuire
Vice President, Production Barbara Schmitz
Production Manager Dominic M. Taormina
Production Coordinator Sarah Katz
IT Manager Denise Donnarumma
Renewal and Billing Manager Nekeya Dancy
Online Subscriptions Manager Jodi Lee

Our Mission Statement
Our goal is for you to enjoy making quilts as much as we do.

LEISURE ARTS STAFF
Vice President of Editorial Susan White Sullivan
Special Projects Director Susan Frantz Wiles
Director of E-Commerce and Prepress Services Mark Hawkins
Imaging Technician Stephanie Johnson
Prepress Technician Janie Marie Wright
Manager of E-Commerce Robert Young

BUSINESS STAFF
President and Chief Executive Officer Rick Barton
Vice President of Sales Mike Behar
Vice President of Finance Laticia Mull Dittrich
Director of Corporate Planning Anne Martin
National Sales Director Martha Adams
Creative Services Chaska Lucas
Information Technology Director Hermine Linz
Controller Francis Caple
Vice President of Operations Jim Dittrich
Retail Customer Service Manager Stan Raynor
Vice President of Purchasing Fred F. Pruss

Library of Congress Control Number: 2012937170
ISBN-13/EAN: 978-1-60900-377-7

10 9 8 7 6 5 4 3 2 1

We're thrilled to bring you this collection of some of our very favorite quilts to delight the young people in your life! The projects we've included are among our most popular of all time. You'll find challenging as well as easy patchwork, plus dashes of fun appliqué. Enjoy the beautiful photography as you browse through the pages to find the quilt that's just right for you. Whether you prefer traditional or contemporary fabrics, you'll find plenty to love. You'll also appreciate our trademarked Sew Easy lessons that will guide you via step-by-step photography through any project-specific special techniques. We predict you'll want to make quilts for all the youngsters in your life!

Happy quilting,

Marianne & Liz

Table of Contents

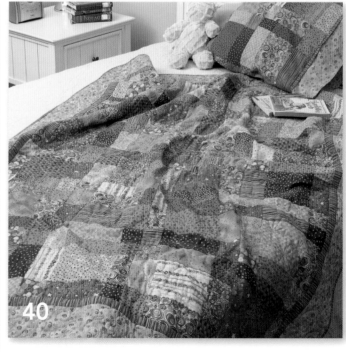

Techniques

124

58

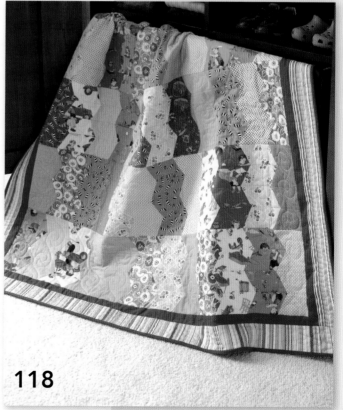

118

Bibbidy Bop

Vibrantly colored squares set on point and surrounded by equally bright, off-kilter borders make this quilt a fun addition to any room.

PROJECT RATING: INTERMEDIATE

Size: 58" × 58"

Blocks: 16 (10") blocks

MATERIALS

2¼ yards yellow print for blocks, sashing, and pieced border

⅞ yard dark blue print for blocks and outer border

¾ yard light green print for blocks and pieced border

¾ yard turquoise print for blocks and middle border

⅝ yard orange print for blocks and pieced border

⅜ yard each red, fuchsia, pink, purple, green, blue, and light turquoise prints for blocks, sashing squares, and pieced border

½ yard red-orange print for binding

3½ yards backing fabric

Twin-size quilt batting

Cutting

Measurements include ¼" seam allowances.

From yellow print, cut:

• 3 (5½"-wide) strips. From strips, cut 20 (5½") squares. Cut squares in half diagonally to make 40 half-square C triangles.

• 1 (4"-wide) strip. From strip, cut 4 (4") squares. Cut squares in half diagonally to make 8 half-square I triangles.

• 5 (3½"-wide) strips. From strips, cut 46 (3½") squares. Cut squares in half diagonally in both directions to make 184 quarter-square H triangles.

• 2 (3"-wide) strips. From strips, cut 18 (3") squares. Cut squares in half diagonally to make 36 half-square G triangles.

• 8 (2¾"-wide) strips. From strips, cut 24 (2¾" × 10½") sashing strips.

• 2 (1¾"-wide) strips. From strips, cut 8 (1¾" × 10") D rectangles.

• 2 (1½"-wide) strips. From strips, cut 8 (1½" × 6") B rectangles.

From dark blue print, cut:

• 7 (3"-wide) strips. Piece strips to make 2 (3" × 58") side outer borders and 2 (3" × 64") top and bottom outer borders.

• 2 (2"-wide) strips. From strips, cut 4 (2" × 12") E rectangles and 10 (2") F squares.

• 2 (1½"-wide) strips. From strips, cut 8 (1½" × 6") B rectangles.

From light green print, cut:

• 2 (5½"-wide) strips. From strips, cut 12 (5½") squares. Cut squares in half diagonally to make 24 half-square C triangles.

• 2 (2"-wide) strips. From strips, cut 4 (2" × 12") E rectangles and 10 (2") F squares.

• 2 (1¾"-wide) strips. From strips, cut 8 (1¾" × 10") D rectangles.

• 2 (1½"-wide) strips. From strips, cut 8 (1½" × 6") B rectangles.

From turquoise print, cut:

• 6 (3"-wide) strips. Piece strips to make 2 (3" × 53") side middle borders and 2 (3" × 59") top and bottom middle borders.

• 1 (2"-wide) strip. From strip, cut 10 (2") F squares.

• 1 (1¾"-wide) strip. From strip, cut 4 (1¾" × 10") D rectangles.

• 2 (1½"-wide) strips. From strips, cut 8 (1½" × 6") B rectangles.

From orange print, cut:
- 2 (4"-wide) strips. From strips, cut 16 (4") A squares.
- 4 (2"-wide) strips. From strips, cut 8 (2" × 12") E rectangles and 10 (2") F squares.
- 2 (1¾"-wide) strips. From strips, cut 8 (1¾" × 10") D rectangles.

From red, fuchsia, pink, purple, green, blue, and light turquoise prints, cut a total of:
- 32 (1½" × 6") B rectangles (8 sets of 4 matching B rectangles).
- 36 (1¾" × 10") D rectangles (9 sets of 4 matching D rectangles).
- 48 (2" × 12") E rectangles (12 sets of 4 matching E rectangles).
- 61 (2") F squares.

From red-orange print, cut:
- 7 (2¼"-wide) strips for binding.

Block Assembly

1. Join matching B rectangles to opposite sides of 1 orange A square as shown in *Round 1 Diagrams*. Trim rectangles at an angle so they are at least ½" wide; trim ends of rectangles even with edges of orange square. Repeat for remaining sides. The center orange square now has an off-kilter narrow border.

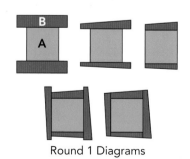

Round 1 Diagrams

2. Add matching C triangles to opposite sides of center as shown in *Round 2 Diagrams*. Repeat for remaining

sides. Trim so sides are not parallel, leaving at least ¼" outside corners of center unit. The orange center square is now turned on point.

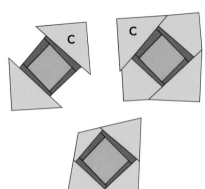

Round 2 Diagrams

3. Join matching D rectangles to opposite sides of center as shown in *Round 3 Diagrams*. Trim rectangles at an angle so they are at least ½" wide; trim ends of strips even with edges of center. Repeat for remaining sides. The center unit now has an off-kilter narrow border.

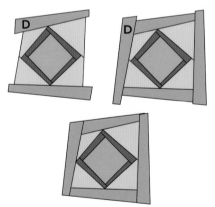

Round 3 Diagrams

4. Add matching E rectangles to opposite sides of block center as shown in *Round 4 Diagrams*. Trim ends of rectangles even with edges of block. Repeat for remaining sides. Trim block to 10½" square. Make 16 blocks, 10 with yellow C triangles and 6 with light green C triangles.

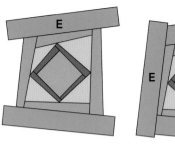

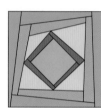

Round 4 Diagrams

5. Referring to *Sashing Square Diagrams*, slightly trim 1 F square so sides are not parallel. Add 2 G triangles to F. Repeat for remaining sides. Trim unit to 2¾" square. Make 9 sashing squares.

Sashing Square Diagrams

Quilt Assembly

1. Lay out blocks, sashing strips, and sashing squares as shown in *Quilt Top Assembly Diagram*. Join into rows; join rows to complete quilt center.

2. Add 2 H triangles to 1 F square as shown in *Border Unit Diagrams*. Trim triangles as shown to complete 1 Border Unit. Make 92 Border Units.

Border Unit Diagrams

3. Referring to *Border Assembly Diagrams*, join 22 Border Units and 2 I triangles to make 1 side border. Make 2 side borders. Trim borders to 3¼" × 47¼" (or length needed to fit quilt). Add borders to sides of quilt center.

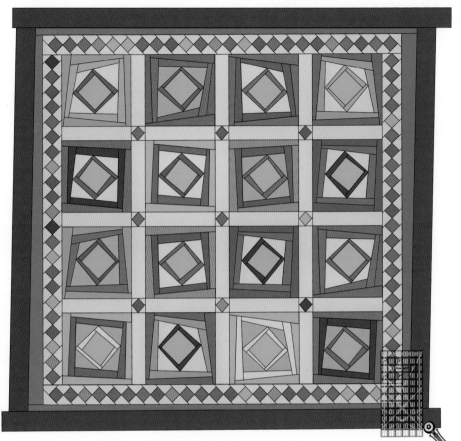

Quilt Top Assembly Diagram

Border Assembly Diagrams

4. Join 24 Border Units and 2 I triangles to make top border. Repeat for bottom border. Trim borders to 3¼" × 52¾" (or length needed to fit quilt). Add borders to quilt.

5. Add turquoise side middle borders to quilt center. Referring to *Quilt Top Assembly Diagram*, trim borders at an angle so they are at least 1" wide; trim ends of borders even with edges of quilt center. Repeat for top and bottom middle borders. The quilt center now has an off-kilter border.

6. Add dark blue side outer borders to quilt center. Trim ends of borders even with edges of quilt. Add dark blue top and bottom outer borders. Square up quilt by cutting 3" outside the seam between the pieced border and middle border as shown in *Quilt Top Assembly Diagram*.

Finishing

1. Divide backing into 2 (1¾-yard) pieces. Cut 1 piece in half lengthwise. Join 1 narrow panel to each side of wider panel; press seam allowances toward narrow panels.

2. Layer backing, batting, and quilt top; baste. Quilt as desired. Quilt shown was quilted with petals radiating from a spiral in the blocks, curved lines in the sashing, and loops, spirals, and curved lines in the borders.

3. Join 2¼"-wide red-orange strips into 1 continuous piece for straight-grain French-fold binding. Add binding to quilt. ✳

QUILT BY **Laura Blanchard.**
MACHINE QUILTED BY **Valerie Schlake.**

Sassy Stars

Quiltmaker Laura Blanchard pieced this cute quilt for a young girl's bed. A special setting trick gives the blocks a little twist.

PROJECT RATING: INTERMEDIATE

Size: 66" × 79"

Blocks: 20 (12") Star blocks

MATERIALS

⅝ yard each of green print, yellow print, and orange print for stars

2½ yards pink print for stars, outer border, and binding

1 fat quarter★ each of turquoise, orange, yellow, pink, and green tone-on-tone fabric for sashing strips

4½ yards purple print for blocks, sashing strips, and inner border

12½" ruled square

5 yards backing fabric

Twin-size quilt batting

★fat quarter = 18" × 20"

Cutting

Measurements include ¼" seam allowances. Border strips are exact length needed. You may want to make them longer to allow for piecing variations.

From each green, yellow, and orange print, cut:

- 1 (5½"-wide) strip. From strip, cut 5 (5½") C squares.
- 4 (3"-wide) strips. From strips, cut 40 (3") A squares.

From pink print, cut:

- 8 (6"-wide) strips. Piece strips to make 2 (6" × 68½") side outer borders and 2 (6" × 66½") top and bottom outer borders.
- 1 (5½"-wide) strip. From strip, cut 5 (5½") C squares.
- 4 (3"-wide) strips. From strips, cut 40 (3") A squares.
- 8 (2¼"-wide) strips for binding.

From each fat quarter, cut:

- 4 (2⅛"-wide) strips for strip sets.

From purple print, cut:

- 3 (16"-wide) strips. From strips, cut 40 (2¾" × 16") D rectangles. Referring to *Triangle Cutting Diagrams*, cut 20 D rectangles in half diagonally to make 40 D1 triangles. Cut 20 D rectangles in half diagonally to make 40 D2 triangles.

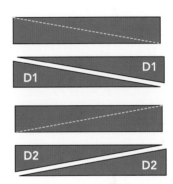

Triangle Cutting Diagrams

- 25 (3"-wide) strips. From strips, cut 160 (3") A squares and 80 (3" × 5½") B rectangles.
- 2 (1½"-wide) strips. From strips, cut 30 (1½") sashing squares.
- 7 (1½"-wide) strips. Piece strips to make 2 (1½" × 66½") side inner borders and 2 (1½" × 55½") top and bottom inner borders.
- 8 (1½"-wide) strips for strip sets. Cut strips in half to make 16 (20"-long) strips.

Block Assembly

1. Choose 1 matching set of 8 print A squares and 1 C square. Referring to *Star Point Unit Diagrams* on page 12, place 1 print A square atop purple

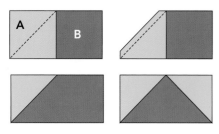

Star Point Unit Diagrams

B rectangle, right sides facing. Stitch diagonally from corner to corner. Trim excess ¼" beyond stitching. Press open to reveal triangle. Repeat for opposite end to complete 1 star point unit. Make 4 star point units.

2. Referring to *Center Unit Diagrams,* place 1 purple A square atop print C square, right sides facing. Stitch diagonally from corner to corner. Trim excess ¼" beyond stitching. Press open to reveal triangle. Repeat for remaining corners to complete center unit.

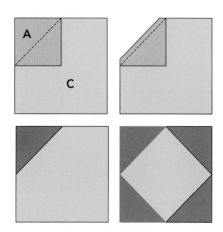

Center Unit Diagrams

3. Lay out 4 star point units, center unit, and 4 purple A squares as shown in *Star Assembly Diagram.* Join pieces into rows; join rows to complete star. Make 20 stars.

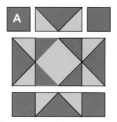

Star Assembly Diagram

4. Lay out stars in 5 rows with 4 stars in each. Place 1 star of each color in each row.

5. When stars are arranged to your liking, tilt them alternately to the left and right as shown in *Quilt Top Assembly Diagram.*

6. For stars that tilt to the left, add D1 triangles; for stars that tilt to the right, add D2 triangles. To make 1 block with star tilted to the left, join 1 D1 triangle to right edge of star, using a partial seam *(Block Assembly Diagrams).* Join 1 D1 triangle to top, left edge, and bottom of star. Complete the partial seam on right edge of block. Using a large square ruler, trim block to 12½". Make 10 blocks with stars that tilt left *(Block Diagrams).* In a similar manner, use D2 triangles to make 10 blocks with stars that tilt to the right.

Sashing Assembly

1. Join 1 (2⅛" × 20") strip of each color tone-on-tone print and 4 (1½" × 20") strips of purple print as shown in *Strip Set Diagram* on page 13. Make 4 strip sets. (Strip sets should measure 12½" high. Trim if necessary.)

2. From strip sets, cut 49 (1½"-wide) segments.

Begin stitching here

Stop stitching here

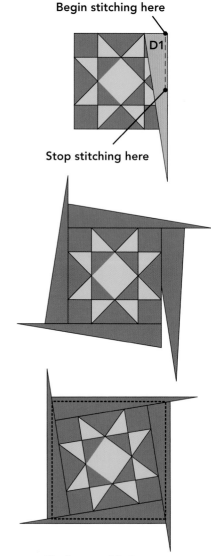

Block Assembly Diagrams

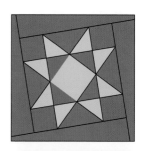

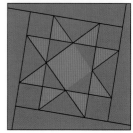

Block Diagrams

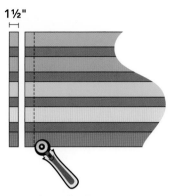

1½"

Strip Set Diagram

Quilt Assembly

1. Lay out blocks, sashing strips, and sashing squares as shown in *Quilt Top Assembly Diagram*. Join pieces into horizontal rows; join rows to complete quilt center.

2. Add purple side inner borders to quilt center. Add purple top and bottom inner borders to quilt.

3. Add pink side outer borders to quilt center. Add pink top and bottom outer borders to quilt.

Finishing

1. Divide backing into 2 (2½-yard) pieces. Divide 1 piece in half lengthwise to make 2 narrow panels. Sew 1 narrow panel to each side of wider panel; press seam allowances toward narrow panels.

2. Layer backing, batting, and quilt top; baste. Quilt as desired. Quilt shown was quilted with an allover meandering pattern of stars and loops.

3. Join 2¼"-wide pink print strips into 1 continuous piece for straight-grain French-fold binding. Add binding to quilt.

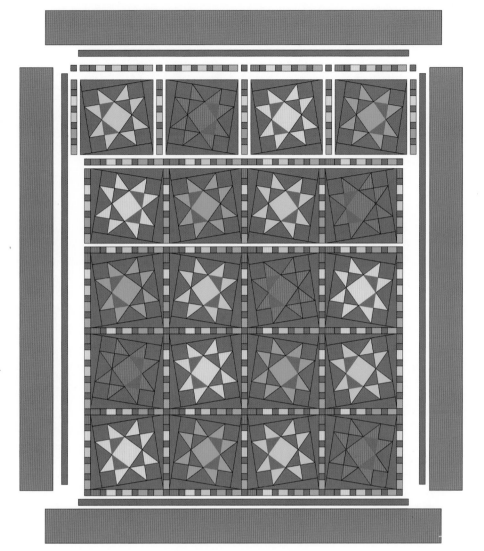

Quilt Top Assembly Diagram

DESIGNER

Laura Blanchard has been quilting since 1986. Her pattern company, Have 2 Quilt, offers patterns for any skill level. Laura also loves teaching a variety of machine technique classes. ✳

QUILT BY **Jean Nolte.**

Tilt-A-Whirl

Everyone loves the rides on the midway, and the classic, not-too-scary Tilt-A-Whirl has been entertaining families for generations. The nine-blade fan units of our polka-dot quilt spin and twirl just like the Tilt-A-Whirl ride. You'll find tips on making the fan units in our Sew Easy lesson on page 19.

PROJECT RATING: INTERMEDIATE

Size: 63" × 63"

Blocks: 32 (8½") Nine-Blade
Fan units

MATERIALS

½ yard each of 12 assorted bright
    polka-dot prints for fan units and
    outer border
2¼ yards bright yellow print for block
    backgrounds and inner border
½ yard red print for setting squares
    and outer border corners
½ yard blue print for binding
Nine-Blade Fan Template Set or
    template material
4 yards backing fabric
Twin-size quilt batting

Cutting

> ### Sew **Smart**™
> Cutting for this quilt is tricky. Be
> sure to read **Sew Easy: Nine-Blade
> Fan Units** on page 19 before
> beginning.

If you do not have the Nine-Blade Fan
Template Set, make templates from patterns on page 17. Measurements include
¼" seam allowances. Border strips are
exact length needed. You may want to
make them longer to allow for piecing
variations.

From each polka-dot print, cut:
• 2 (2"-wide) strips. From strips, cut 12
  (2" × 5") rectangles for outer border.
• 24 fan blades.

From bright yellow print, cut:
• 6 (2"-wide) strips. Piece strips to make
  2 (2" × 51½") side inner borders and
  2 (2" × 54½") top and bottom inner
  borders.
• 32 fan background pieces.

TILT·A·WHIRL

From red print, cut:

- 1 (8½"-wide) strip. From strip, cut 4 (8½") setting squares.
- 1 (5"-wide) strip. From strip, cut 4 (5") squares for border corners.

From blue print, cut:

- 7 (2¼"-wide) strips for binding.

Fan Unit Assembly

1. Refer to *Sew Easy: Nine-Blade Fan Units* on page 19 to complete 1 fan unit *(Fan Unit Diagram)*.

Fan Unit Diagram

2. Make 32 fan units.

Quilt Assembly

1. Lay out fan units and setting squares as shown in *Quilt Top Assembly Diagram*. Join into horizontal rows; join rows to complete quilt center.

2. Add yellow print side inner borders to quilt center. Add yellow print top and bottom inner borders to quilt.

3. Join 36 assorted polka-dot rectangles to make 1 outer border. Make 4 outer borders.

4. Add 1 outer border to each side of quilt center. Add 1 red print border corner square to each end of remaining outer borders. Add borders to top and bottom of quilt.

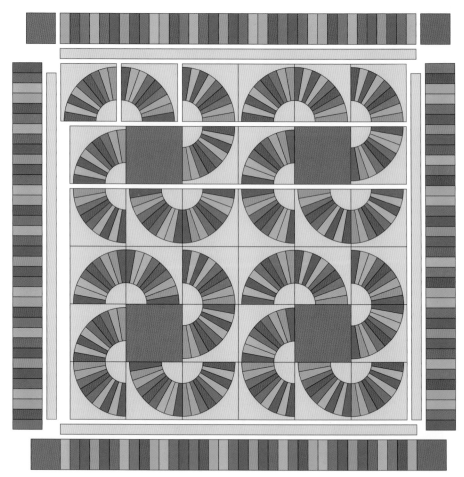

Quilt Top Assembly Diagram

Finishing

1. Divide backing fabric into 2 (2-yard) pieces. Divide 1 piece in half lengthwise to make 2 narrow panels. Sew 1 narrow panel to each side of wider panel; press seam allowances toward narrow panels.

2. Layer backing, batting, and quilt top; baste. Quilt as desired. Quilt shown was quilted with arcs in the fan units, loops in the block background and inner border, concentric circles in the setting squares and border corner squares, and in the ditch in the outer border.

3. Join 2¼"-wide blue print strips into 1 continuous piece for straight-grain French-fold binding. Add binding to quilt.

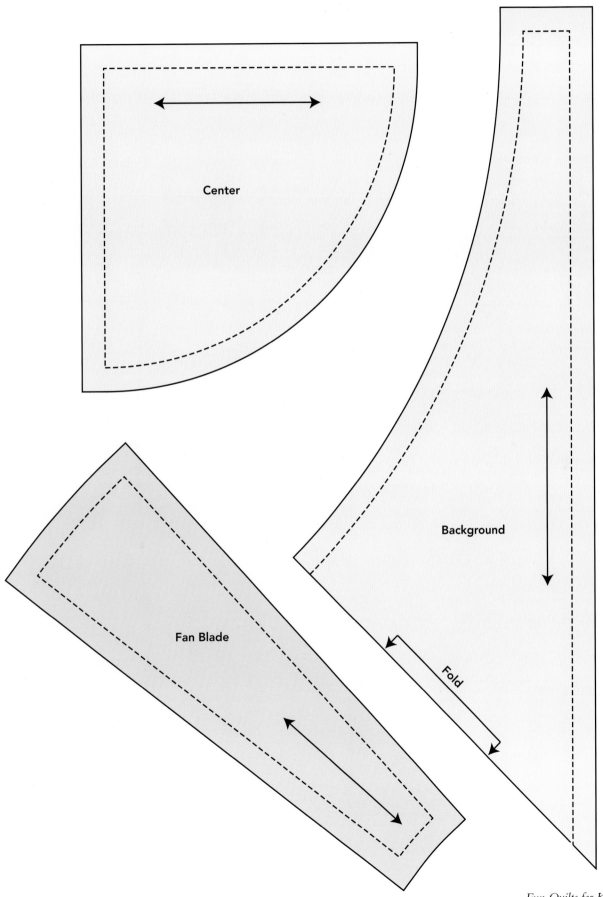

Center

Background

Fan Blade

Fold

TRIED & TRUE

For a different look, use a dark background and light fan blades from fabrics like these from the Shadow Play collection by Maywood Studio. ✳

Nine-Blade Fan Units

Using our Nine-Blade Fan Template Set and a small rotary cutter makes cutting the pieces for 8½" fan units fast and easy. Stitch fan units into the *Tilt-A-Whirl* quilt on page 14, or create a design of your own.

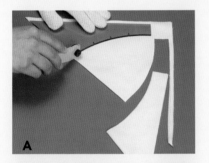

A

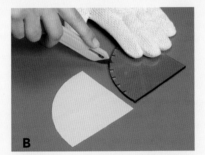

B

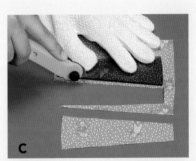

C

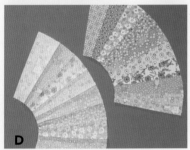

D

E

F

Cutting

1. From background fabric, cut 10½"-wide strips. From strips, cut 10½" squares. You can cut 2 background pieces from each square.

2. Fold background square in half diagonally. Align fold edge of template with fold of background square and cut 1 background piece. Flip template over and cut a second piece from background square *(Photo A)*. Use a point cutting tool to mark the notches in background pieces.

3. Using center template, cut 1 center piece for each fan unit. Use a point cutting tool to mark the notches *(Photo B)*.

4. Cut 5½"-wide strips from fabrics for blades. Cut 9 blades for each fan unit, using blade template and rotating it on strip after each cut *(Photo C)*.

Assembly

1. Join 9 fan blades. Press all seam allowances in one direction *(Photo D)*.

2. Place blade unit atop center piece, right sides together. Align seams in blade unit with notches in center piece. Place a pin at each end and at 1 or 2 of the notches in center of piece. With blade unit on top, stitch ¼" seam *(Photo E)*. Press seam allowance toward center piece.

3. Place background piece atop blade unit, right sides together. Align seams in blade unit with notches in background piece. Place a pin at each end and at 1 or 2 of the notches in center of piece. With background piece on top, stitch ¼" seam *(Photo F)*. Press seam allowance toward background piece.

Spin Cycle

Designer Bethany Reynolds combined fabric she designed and her Stack-n-Whack® method to create this fun contemporary quilt. See *Sew Easy: Cutting Kaleidoscope Pieces* on page 23 to learn her cutting technique.

PROJECT RATING: INTERMEDIATE

Size: 60½" × 85½"

Blocks: 24 (9") Kaleidoscope blocks

MATERIALS

3 yards multicolor print for blocks
(or enough to cut 8 (11"-long)
or longer repeats of pattern in
fabric)

2 yards white print for sashing and
block background

1 yard spiral dot print for sashing

¾ yard bright circle print

2⅜ yards stripe for border

⅝ yard turquoise print for binding

5¼ yards backing fabric

Twin-size quilt batting

Cutting

NOTE: Cutting the kite-shaped pieces
for the blocks in this quilt requires a
special technique. See *Sew Easy: Cutting
Kaleidoscope Pieces* on page 23 for
instructions.

Measurements include ¼" seam allowances. Border strips are exact length needed. You may want to make them longer to allow for piecing variations.

From multicolor print, cut:

• 24 sets of 8 matching A kite pieces.
(See *Sew Easy: Cutting Kaleidoscope Pieces* on page 23.)

From white print, cut:

• 5 (3½"-wide) strips. From strips cut 48 (3½") squares. Cut squares in half diagonally to make 96 half-square B triangles.

• 30 (1½"-wide) strips for strip sets.

From spiral dot print, cut:

• 15 (2"-wide) strips for strip sets.

From bright circle print, cut:

• 39 (4") sashing squares, centering a spiral in each square.

From stripe, cut:

• 4 (4"-wide) **lengthwise** strips, centering the same portion of stripe print in each one. From strips, cut 2 (4" × 79") side borders and 2 (4" × 54") top and bottom borders.

From turquoise print, cut:

• 8 (2¼"-wide) strips for binding.

Block Assembly

1. Choose 1 stack of 8 identical A pieces. Referring to *Block Assembly Diagram*, join 2 pieces to make a pair; repeat to make 4 pairs. Join 2 pairs to make a half block. Make 2 half blocks; join to complete Kaleidoscope block center.

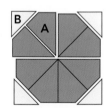

Block Assembly Diagram

2. Add 1 B triangle to each corner to complete 1 block (*Block Diagram*). Make 24 blocks.

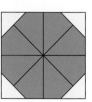

Block Diagram

Quilt Assembly

1. Join 2 (1½"-wide) white print strips
   and 1 (2"-wide) spiral dot print strip
   as shown in *Strip Set Diagram*. Make
   15 strip sets. Press seam allowances toward spiral print. From strip sets, cut 58
   (9½"-wide) segments for sashing strips.

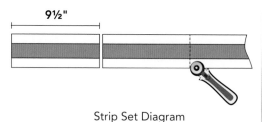

9½"

Strip Set Diagram

2. Lay out blocks, sashing strips, and
   sashing squares as shown in photo.
   Join into horizontal rows; join rows
   to complete quilt center.
3. Add side borders to quilt center.
4. Join 1 sashing square to each end of
   top and bottom borders. Add borders
   to quilt.

Finishing

1. Divide backing into 2 (2⅝-yard)
   pieces. Cut 1 piece in half lengthwise to make 2 narrow panels. Join
   1 narrow panel to each side of wider
   panel; press seam allowances toward
   narrow panel.
2. Layer backing, batting, and quilt top;
   baste. Quilt as desired. Quilt shown
   has an overall freehand design in the
   blocks, outline quilting on spirals in
   sashing squares, and a zigzag pattern
   in the border.
3. Join 2¼"-wide turquoise print strips
   into 1 continuous piece for straight-
   grain French-fold binding. Add
   binding to quilt.

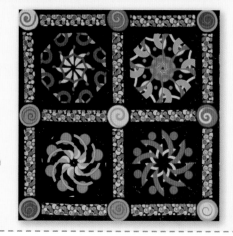

TRIED & TRUE

Bethany's GeoMagic fabric
collection is also available
in bright colors with a black
background. She used that
colorway to make this version
of her *Spin Cycle* quilt.

Sew Easy™

Cutting Kaleidoscope Pieces

Bethany Reynolds developed her Stack-n-Whack® method for cutting identical pieces to make kaleidoscope blocks. This popular technique makes quick work of the cutting process.

A

B

C

Making the Stack

1. Cut kaleidoscope fabric in half lengthwise.
2. Straighten end of one half-width of fabric. Focusing on a specific motif in fabric, cut a strip that is the width of one pattern repeat (approximately 12" for the GeoMagic print used in *Spin Cycle*). Using this piece as a guide, cut 7 more strips, each 1 pattern repeat wide (*Photo A*).
3. Press and then stack the 8 layers so that motifs are perfectly lined up. Pin the layers in several places to keep them from slipping when cutting.

Sew **Smart**™
Push a flathead pin through each layer in exactly the same spot on the print to align layers as shown in *Photo B*. — Marianne

4. Repeat steps #2 and #3 to make a second 8-layer stack from the remaining piece of fabric.

Cutting Kite-shaped Pieces

1. From each stack, cut 2 (5⅜"-wide) strips. From strips, cut 12 (5⅜") squares.

2. Cut each stack of squares in half diagonally to make 24 half-square triangle stacks.
3. To cut each triangle stack into a kite shape, place the 5⅜" line of ruler on bottom left corner of triangle stack; cut off corner to make 8 A kite pieces (*Photo C*).

DESIGNER

Bethany Reynolds has a knack for finding ways to get great results with less work and loves sharing her tricks. She has published numerous patterns for quilts and wearable art, has developed a line of Stack-n-Whack® specialty rulers, and has written three books on her Stack-n-Whack method.

Bethany grew up on Mount Desert Island in Maine and currently lives nearby on the mainland. When not quilting or working at the computer, she enjoys cooking, visiting Acadia National Park with her family, or settling in with a good book. ❋

Summer Flip-Flops

Make this playful quilt using your brightest, wildest prints.
Everybody loves flip-flops!

PROJECT RATING: INTERMEDIATE
Size: 52" × 62"
Blocks: 20 (8" × 9½")
Flip-Flop blocks
40 (5") Log Cabin blocks

MATERIALS

20 fat eighths★ assorted bright
  prints for flip-flops
1½ yards cream print
7 fat quarters★★ assorted plaids and
  dots in pink, orange, and purple
4 fat quarters★★ assorted yellow
  prints
⅜ yard yellow print #1 for border
½ yard yellow print #2 for binding
3½ yards backing fabric
Paper-backed fusible web
Twin-size quilt batting
★fat eighth = 9" × 20"
★★fat quarter = 18" × 20"

Cutting

Measurements include ¼" seam
allowances. Border strips are exact
length needed. You may want to make
them longer to allow for piecing variations.
Appliqué patterns are on page 29.
Follow manufacturer's instructions for
using fusible web.

**From each bright print fat
  eighth, cut:**
• 1 Sole.
• 1 Sole reversed.
• 1 Strap.
• 1 Strap reversed.

From cream print, cut:
• 5 (10"-wide) strips. From strips, cut 20
  (8½" × 10") background rectangles.

**From each plaid/dot fat
  quarter, cut:**
• 10 (1½"-wide) strips. Set 32 strips
  aside for strip sets. From remaining
  strips, cut:
  36 (1½" × 5½")
  E rectangles, 36 (1½" × 4½")
  D rectangles, 36 (1½" × 3½") C
  rectangles, 36 (1½" × 2½")
  B rectangles, and 36 (1½") A squares.

From each yellow print fat quarter, cut:

- 8 (1½"-wide) strips. From strips, cut
  4 (1½" × 5½") E rectangles,
  44 (1½" × 4½") D rectangles,
  44 (1½" × 3½") C rectangles,
  44 (1½" × 2½") B rectangles, and
  44 (1½") A squares.

From yellow print #1, cut:

- 6 (1½"-wide) strips. Piece strips to make 2 (1½" × 52½") top and bottom outer borders and 2 (1½" × 60½") side outer borders.

From yellow print #2, cut:

- 7 (2¼"-wide) strips for binding.

Block Assembly

1. Position appliqué pieces on background rectangle as shown in *Flip-Flop Block Diagram*.

Flip-Flop Block Diagram

2. Fuse pieces in place and machine zigzag edges of appliqué using matching thread. Make 20 Flip-Flop blocks.

3. Referring to *Log Cabin Block A Diagrams*, join 1 yellow A square and 1 plaid A square. Continue adding pieces in alphabetical order to complete 1 block. Make 36 Log Cabin Block A.

Log Cabin Block A Diagrams

4. In the same manner, make 4 Log Cabin Block B using yellow print squares and rectangles *(Log Cabin Block B Diagram)*.

Log Cabin Block B Diagram

Sashing Assembly

1. Join 4 (1½"-wide) plaid and dot strips as shown in *Strip Set Diagram*. Make 8 Strip Sets. From strip sets, cut 40 (3½"-wide) segments.

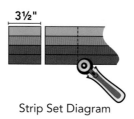

Strip Set Diagram

2. Referring to *Quilt Top Assembly Diagram*, join 10 strip set segments to make 1 sashing row. Make 4 sashing rows.

Quilt Assembly

1. Lay out Flip-Flop blocks and sashing rows as shown in *Quilt Top Assembly Diagram* on page 27. Join blocks into rows; join rows to complete quilt center.

2. Join 10 Log Cabin Block A to make 1 Side inner border. Make 2 Side inner borders. In the same manner, join 8 Log Cabin Block A and 2 Log Cabin Block B to make top inner border. Repeat for bottom inner border.

3. Add side inner borders to quilt center. Add top and bottom inner borders to quilt.

4. Repeat for yellow print outer borders.

Finishing

1. Divide backing into 2 (1¾-yard) lengths. Join panels lengthwise. Seam will run horizontally.

2. Layer backing, batting, and quilt top; baste. Quilt as desired. Quilt shown was quilted with meandering in the background, swirls in the sashing, a sun design in the Log Cabin blocks, and a curved line in the outer border *(Quilting Diagram)*.

3. Join 2¼"-wide yellow print strips into 1 continuous piece for straight-grain French-fold binding. Add binding to quilt.

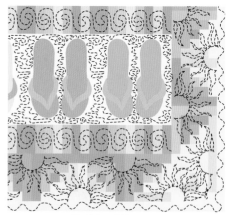

Quilting Diagram

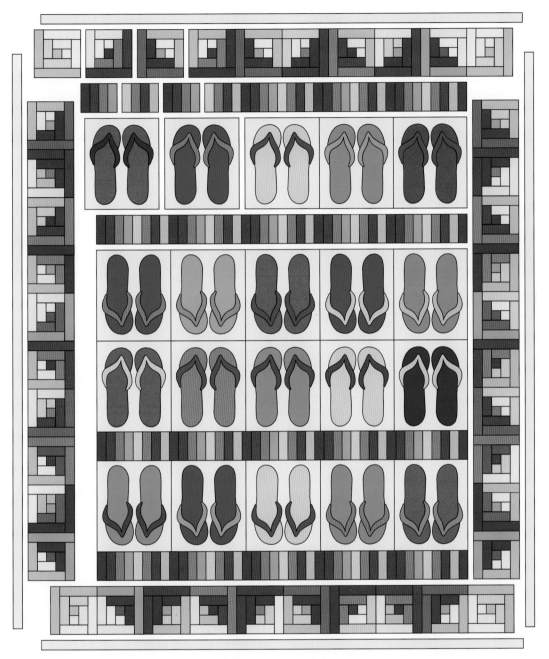

Quilt Top Assembly Diagram

DESIGNER

Carol Burniston likes to make quilts using bright, fun colors that make her smile. Look for Carol's books, *Color-Splashed Quilts* and *Wonderfully Whimsical Quilts*, published by C&T Publishing, at your local quilt store. ✳

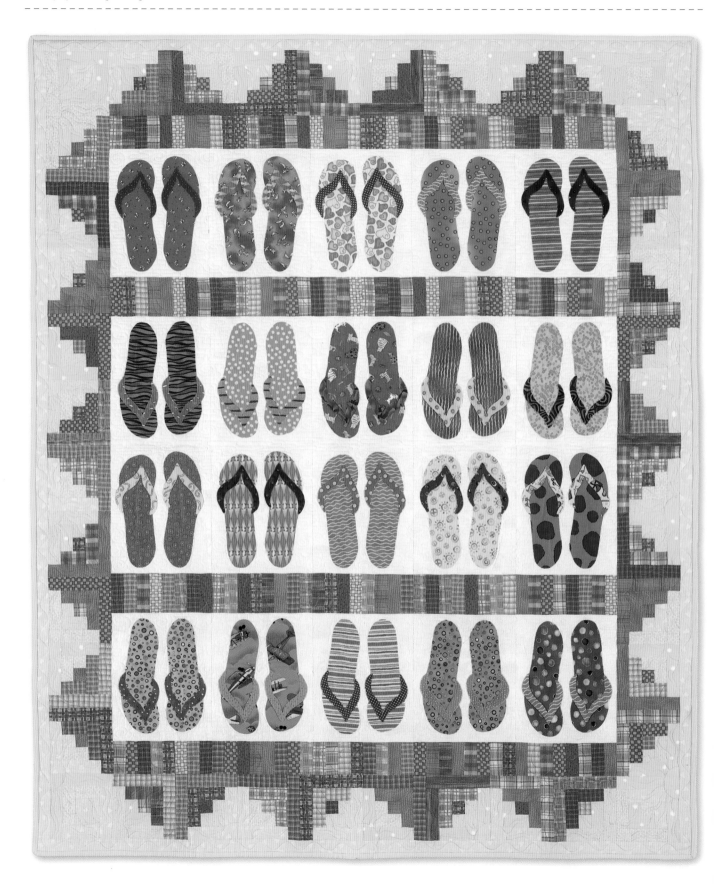

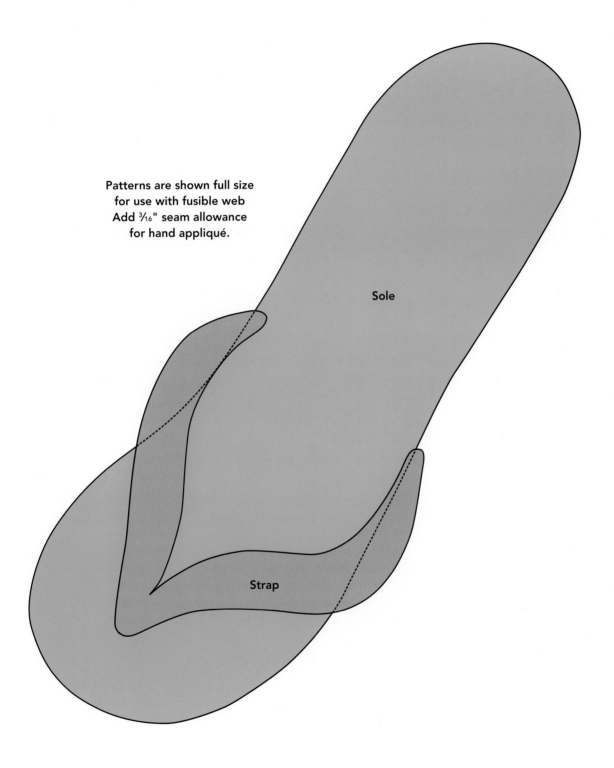

Patterns are shown full size
for use with fusible web
Add ³⁄₁₆" seam allowance
for hand appliqué.

Sole

Strap

Something Fishy

Patricia Harrop won several small fish blocks at a Smoky Mountain Quilter's Guild meeting. She designed additional larger fish, stitching them with novelty fabrics. "Many of the blocks are a pun," says Patricia. "For example, I used a cat print to make catfish, and other appropriate prints to make neon fish, convict fish, jellyfish, sunfish, and starfish. Just for fun, I also used holiday fabrics."

PROJECT RATING: INTERMEDIATE

Size: 68" × 110½"

Blocks: 18 (12") Big Fish blocks
36 (6") Small Fish blocks

MATERIALS

18 (6½") A squares assorted prints for big fish bodies

18 (4¾" × 20") strips assorted prints for big fish fins and heads

18 (8" × 12") strips assorted prints for small fish

14 (3⅞" × 13") strips assorted blue and green prints for small fish backgrounds

3¾ yards light blue print for background

1 yard dark green print

1 yard blue wave print for outer border

¾ yard bright stripe for binding

6½ yards backing fabric

King-size batting

Cutting

Measurements include ¼" seam allowances. Fins and head match for most Big Fish blocks. Most bodies and tails for Small Fish blocks match. Mix or match fabrics as desired.

From each strip for big fish fins and heads, cut:

• 4 (4¾") B squares.

From each strip for small fish, cut:

• 1 (6⅞") square. Cut square in half diagonally to make 2 half-square C triangles.

• 1 (3⅞") square. Cut square in half diagonally to make 2 half-square D triangles.

From each strip for small fish backgrounds, cut:

• 3 (3⅞") squares. Cut squares in half diagonally to make 6 half-square D triangles.

From light blue print, cut:

• 18 (6½"-wide) strips. From strips, cut 102 (6½") A squares.

• 2 (3⅞"-wide) strips. From strips, cut 12 (3⅞") squares. Cut squares in half diagonally to make 24 half-square D triangles for 8 Small Fish Blocks.

From dark green print, cut:

• 5 (6½"-wide) strips. From strips; cut 30 (6½") A squares.

From blue wave print, cut:

• 3 (9¾"-wide) strips. From strips; cut 11 (9¾") squares. Cut squares in half diagonally in both directions to make 44 quarter-square triangles for outer border (2 are extra.)

From bright stripe, cut:

• 10 (2¼"-wide) strips for binding.

Big Fish Block Assembly

1. Choose 3 light blue print A squares, 1 print A square, and 4 matching B squares.

2. Referring to *Diagonal Seams Diagrams*, place 1 B square atop 1 blue A square. Stitch diagonally from corner to corner. Trim ¼" beyond stitching. Press open to reveal triangle to complete 1 unit. Make 3 units with blue print A squares and 1 unit with print A square.

Diagonal Seams Diagrams

3. Lay out units as shown in *Big Fish Block Assembly Diagram*. Join to complete 1 Big Fish block *(Big Fish Block Diagram)*. Make 18 Big Fish blocks.

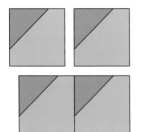

Big Fish Block Assembly Diagram

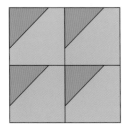

Big Fish Block Diagram

Small Fish Block Assembly

1. Choose 1 set of matching C and D triangles and 3 matching D triangles.

2. Referring to *Small Fish Block Assembly Diagram*, join triangles to conplete 1 Small Fish block *(Small Fish Block Diagram)*.

Small Fish Block Assembly Diagram

Small Fish Block Diagram

3. Make 28 Small Fish blocks with assorted print backgrounds. Make 8 Small Fish blocks for top and bottom of quilt using light blue background D triangles.

Quilt Assembly

1. Lay out Big Fish blocks, Small Fish blocks, dark green print A squares, light blue print A squares, and outer border triangles as shown in *Quilt Top Assembly Diagram*.

Section 2 Section 1

A

Section 4 Section 3

Quilt Top Assembly Diagram

2. Join into 4 sections as shown in *Quilt Top Assembly Diagram.*

3. Join Sections to complete quilt top.

Quilting and Finishing

1. Divide backing into 2 (3¼-yard) lengths. Cut 1 piece in half lengthwise to make 2 narrow panels. Join 1 narrow panel to each side of wider panel. Press seam allowances toward narrow panels.

2. Layer backing, batting, and quilt top; baste. Quilt as desired. Quilt shown was outline quilted around fish. Background is quilted with waves, bubbles, and seaweed.

3. Join 2¼"-wide bright stripe strips into 1 continuous piece for straight-grain French-fold binding. Add binding to quilt.

DESIGNER

Patricia Harrop of Knoxville, Tennessee enjoys several hobbies including endurance horseback riding, embroidery, painting, sculpture, and snow skiing. ✳

QUILT DESIGNED AND MACHINE QUILTED BY **Cyndi Walker**.
MADE BY **Debbie Gray**.

Rainbow Jamboree

Make this fun, bright quilt with its matching tote bag and teach kids about the environment at the same time! Fabrics include messages about "going green" and show happy, smiling faces of kids making a difference.

PROJECT RATING: EASY

Size: 48" × 64"
Blocks: 24 (8") Hourglass blocks
24 (8") Puss in the Corner blocks

MATERIALS

½ yard kids print
⅝ yard pink print
½ yard pink geometric print
½ yard blue geometric print
⅜ yard orange geometric print
1 fat quarter★ purple dots
⅜ yard green dots
⅝ yard pink dots
⅜ yard yellow dots
⅜ yard green large earth print
⅜ yard yellow large earth print
¼ yard yellow small earth print
½ yard purple small earth print
½ yard pink-and-blue stripe for binding
3 yards backing fabric
Twin-size quilt batting
★fat quarter = 18" × 20"

Cutting

Measurements include ¼" seam allowances.

From kids print, cut:
- 3 (4½"-wide) strips. From strips, cut 24 (4½") B squares.

From pink print, cut:
- 2 (9¼"-wide) strips. From strips, cut 5 (9¼") squares. Cut squares in half diagonally in both directions to make 20 quarter-square A triangles.

From pink geometric print, cut:
- 3 (4½"-wide) strips. From strips, cut 48 (4½" × 2½") C rectangles.

From blue geometric print, cut:
- 3 (4½"-wide) strips. From strips, cut 48 (4½" × 2½") C rectangles.

From orange geometric print, cut:
- 1 (9¼"-wide) strip. From strip, cut 3 (9¼") squares. Cut squares in half diagonally in both directions to make 12 quarter-square A triangles.

From purple dots fat quarter, cut:
- 1 (9¼") square. Cut square in half diagonally in both directions to make 4 quarter-square A triangles.

From green dots, cut:
- 1 (9¼"-wide) strip. From strip, cut 3 (9¼") squares. Cut squares in half diagonally in both directions to make 12 quarter-square A triangles.

From pink dots, cut:
- 2 (9¼"-wide) strips. From strips, cut 5 (9¼") squares. Cut squares in half diagonally in both directions to make 20 quarter-square A triangles.

From yellow dots, cut:
- 3 (2½"-wide) strips. From strips, cut 48 (2½") D squares.

From green large earth print, cut:
- 1 (9¼"-wide) strip. From strip, cut 3 (9¼") squares. Cut squares in half diagonally in both directions to make 12 quarter-square A triangles.

From yellow large earth print, cut:
- 1 (9¼"-wide) strip. From strip, cut 3 (9¼") squares. Cut squares in half diagonally in both directions to make 12 quarter-square A triangles.

From yellow small earth print, cut:
- 2 (2½"-wide) strips. From strips, cut 32 (2½") D squares.

From purple small earth print, cut:

- 1 (9¼") strip. From strip, cut 1 (9¼") square. Cut square in half diagonally in both directions to make 4 quarter-square A triangles.
- 1 (2½"-wide) strip. From strip, cut 16 (2½") D squares.

From pink and blue stripe, cut:

- 6 (2¼"-wide) strips for binding.

Hourglass Block Assembly

1. Join 2 purple small earth print A triangles and 2 purple dots A triangles to make 1 Hourglass block *(Hourglass Block Diagrams)*. Make 2 purple Hourglass blocks.

Hourglass Block Diagrams

2. In the same manner, make 6 green Hourglass blocks using green large earth print A triangles and green dots A triangles. Make 10 pink Hourglass blocks using pink print A triangles and pink dots A triangles. Make 6 Hourglass blocks using yellow large earth print A triangles and orange geometric print A triangles.

Puss in the Corner Block Assembly

1. Lay out 1 kids print B square, 4 blue geometric print C rectangles, and 4 purple small earth print D squares as shown in *Puss in the Corner Block Assembly Diagram*. Join to make 1 Puss in the Corner block *(Puss in the Corner Block Diagram)*. Make 4 matching Puss in the Corner blocks.

2. In the same manner, make 8 Puss in the corner blocks using kids print

B squares, blue geometric print C rectangles, and yellow small earth print D squares. Make 12 Puss in the Corner blocks using kids print B squares, pink geometric print C rectangles, and yellow dots D squares.

Quilt Assembly

1. Lay out blocks as shown in *Quilt Top Assembly Diagram*.
2. Join into rows; join rows to complete quilt top.

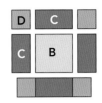

Puss in the Corner
Block Assembly Diagram

Puss in the Corner Block Diagram

Quilt Top Assembly Diagram

Quilting Diagram

DESIGNER

Cyndi Walker is a quilt designer, teacher, and author who lives near Seattle, Washington. Her pattern company, Stitch Studios, features original, fun and easy quilt patterns that incorporate her love for scrap quilts and appliqué. Look for her book, *Spotlight on Scraps*, published by Martingale & Company. ✳

Finishing

1. Divide backing into 2 (1½-yard) lengths. Join panels lengthwise. Seam will run horizontally.

2. Layer backing, batting, and quilt top; baste. Quilt as desired. Quilt shown was quilted with an allover design of swirls and feathers (*Quilting Diagram*).

3. Join 2¼"-wide pink-and-blue stripe strips into 1 continuous piece for straight-grain French-fold binding. Add binding to quilt.

SIZE OPTIONS

	Crib (40" × 56")	Twin (72" × 88")	Full (88" × 104")
Blocks	35	99	143
Setting	5 × 7	9 × 11	11 × 13

MATERIALS

	Crib (40" × 56")	Twin (72" × 88")	Full (88" × 104")
Kids Print	½ yard	1 yard	1¼ yards
Pink Print	⅜ yard	⅝ yard	1 yard
Pink Geometric Print	½ yard	¾ yard	1 yard
Blue Geometric Print	⅜ yard	1¼ yards	1¾ yards
Orange Geometric Print	⅜ yard	⅝ yard	⅝ yard
Purple Dots	—	⅜ yard	⅝ yard
Green Dots	⅜ yard	⅝ yard	1 yard
Pink Dots	⅜ yard	⅝ yard	1 yard
Yellow Dots	⅜ yard	⅝ yard	⅝ yard
Green Large Earth Print	⅜ yard	⅝ yard	1 yard
Yellow Large Earth Print	⅜ yard	⅝ yard	⅝ yard
Yellow Small Earth Print	¼ yard	⅜ yard	½ yard
Purple Small Earth Print	⅛ yard	⅜ yard	½ yard
Pink and Blue Stripe	½ yard	¾ yard	⅞ yard
Backing Fabric	2½ yards	5¼ yards	8 yards
Batting	Crib-size	Full-size	Queen-size

WEB EXTRA

Go to www.FonsandPorter.com/rainbowsizes to download *Quilt Top Assembly Diagrams* for these size options.

Kids Go Green Tote

Make a bag to carry your quilt or to use as an eco-friendly shopping bag.

Size: 18½" × 11½"

MATERIALS

1 Bag panel

OR

¾ yard blue print for bag

1 fat eighth★ contrasting print for pocket

⅝ yard multicolor print for handles and bottom

⅛ yard binding fabric

★fat eighth = 9" × 20"

Cutting

Measurements include ¼" seam allowances.

NOTE: If using panel print, cut all pieces on outer lines. If not using panel print, cut the following pieces:

From blue print, cut:
- 1 (19"-wide) strip. From strip, cut 1 (19" × 28½") rectangle.

From contrasting print, cut:
- 1 (7½"-wide) strip. From strip, cut 1 (7½") square for pocket.

From mulitcolor print, cut:
- 1 (10½"-wide) strip. From strip, cut 1 (10½" × 19") rectangle for bottom.
- 2 (3¾" × 41") strips.

From binding fabric, cut:
- 2 (2¼"-wide) strips.

Bag Assembly

1. Double hem top edge of pocket square. Topstitch hem.
2. Center pocket on bag rectangle, 2½" from top edge as shown in *Pocket Placement Diagram*. Baste pocket to bag rectangle along bottom and side edges.

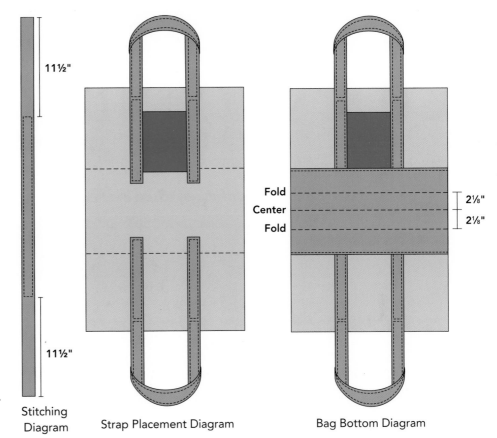

Stitching Diagram · Strap Placement Diagram · Bag Bottom Diagram

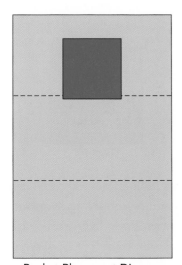

Pocket Placement Diagram

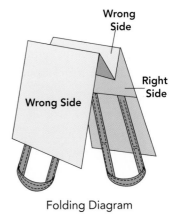

Folding Diagram

3. Press strap seam allowances on long sides toward wrong side. Press straps in half lengthwise. Pin together, marking straps with a pin 11½" from each end.
4. Stitch between pins as shown in *Stitching Diagram*. Repeat for second strap.
5. Position straps on bag rectangle, covering side edges of pocket and placing ends of straps 1½" below bottom of pocket as shown in *Strap Placement Diagram*. Stitch straps to bag.
6. Press seam allowance on long sides of bottom rectangle toward wrong side. Center bottom rectangle atop bag rectangle, covering bottom of pocket and ends of straps. Topstitch ⅛" from edges of bottom rectangle *(Bag Bottom Diagram)*. Make marks in seam allowance at center of bottom and 2⅛" away from center mark on each side.
7. With right sides facing, fold bag accordian-style at marks *(Folding Diagram)*. Stitch side seams; zigzag or serge seams. Turn bag right side out.
8. Join 2¼"-wide binding strips into 1 continuous piece for straight-grain French-fold binding. Add binding to top of bag.

Uneven Nine Patch

This free-form cutting technique is a fun way to use a variety of fabric squares. Pay careful attention as you cut and stack fabrics, and you'll have this quilt done in no time.

PROJECT RATING: EASY

Size: 50" × 70"

Blocks: 24 (10") Uneven Nine Patch blocks

MATERIALS

27 (12") squares assorted prints

¾ yard multicolor stripe for inner border and binding

1 yard pink print for outer border

12½" rotary cutting square ruler

3¼ yards backing fabric

Twin-size quilt batting

Cutting

Measurements include ¼" seam allowances. Border strips are exact length needed. You may want to make them longer to allow for piecing variations.

From multicolor stripe, cut:

• 7 (2¼"-wide) strips for binding.

• 6 (1½"-wide) strips. Piece strips to make 2 (1½" × 60½") side inner borders and 2 (1½" × 42½") top and bottom inner borders.

From pink print, cut:

• 7 (4½"-wide) strips. Piece strips to make 2 (4½" × 62½") side outer borders and 2 (4½" × 50½") top and bottom outer borders.

Block Assembly

1. Stack 9 squares, right sides up, aligning all edges. Using rotary cutter and ruler, make 1 diagonal cut through stack at least 1" from edge as shown in *Diagram 1*.

> ### Sew **Smart**™
> To make cutting through 9 layers of fabric easier, use a large (60mm) rotary cutter. —Marianne

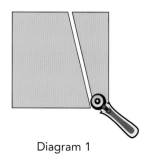

Diagram 1

2. Move top small piece to bottom of stack.

3. Join 2 top pieces from stack *(Diagram 2)*. Continue chain piecing all pairs of pieces in stack.

Diagram 2

4. Cut chain threads and press seam allowances toward smaller pieces. Restack blocks in original order.

5. Make cut #2 at least 1" away from edge as shown in *Diagram 3*.

Diagram 3

6. Put the top **2** small pieces at the bottom of the stack. Chain piece pairs of pieces in stack. Press seams toward

smaller pieces. Restack blocks in original order.

7. Rotate stack 90 degrees and make cut #3 *(Diagram 4)*. Place the top **3** smaller pieces at the bottom of the stack and join pairs of pieces as shown in *Diagram 5*.

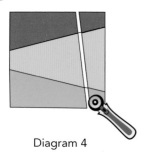

Diagram 4

Diagram 5

8. Make cut #4 *(Diagram 6)*. Place top **6** smaller pieces at the bottom of the stack and join pairs of pieces to complete block as shown in *Block Diagram*.

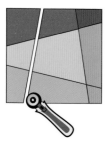

Diagram 6

Block Diagram

9. You will have 9 Uneven Nine Patch blocks, each made of 9 different fabrics. Trim blocks to 10½" with rotary cutting square ruler.

10. Repeat steps #1–#9 two more times to make a total of 27 blocks. (You will have 3 extra blocks.)

Quilt Assembly

1. Lay out blocks as shown in *Quilt Top Assembly Diagram*.

2. Join blocks into rows; join rows to complete quilt center.

3. Add stripe side inner borders to quilt center. Add top and bottom inner borders to quilt. Repeat for pink print outer borders.

Finishing

1. Divide backing into 2 (1⅝-yard) lengths. Join pieces lengthwise. Seam will run horizontally.

2. Layer backing, batting, and quilt top; baste. Quilt as desired. Quilt shown was quilted with a fireworks design in blocks and a swirl pattern in outer border *(Quilting Diagram)*.

3. Join 2¼"-wide stripe strips into 1 continuous piece for straight-grain French-fold binding. Add binding to quilt.

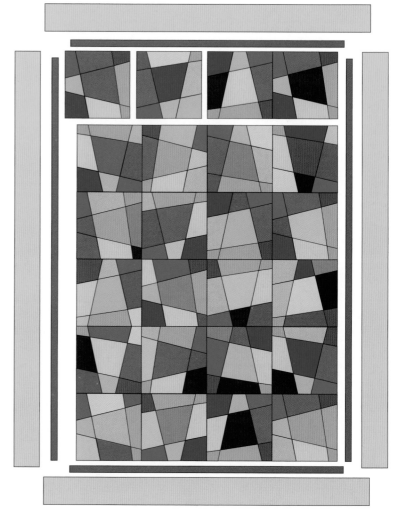

Quilt Top Assembly Diagram

SIZE OPTIONS

	Crib (40" × 40")	Twin (60" × 90")	Full (80" × 100")
Blocks	9 blocks	40 blocks	63 blocks
Setting	3 × 3 blocks	5 × 8 blocks	7 × 9 blocks

MATERIALS

	Crib (40" × 40")	Twin (60" × 90")	Full (80" × 100")
Assorted print squares	9 (12") squares	45 (12") squares	63 (12") squares
Stripe for border and binding	½ yard	1 yard	1¼ yards
Pink print for outer border and binding fabric	⅝ yard	1⅛ yards	1⅜ yards
Backing fabric	2⅝ yards	5½ yards	7½ yards
Batting	Crib-size	Full-size	Queen-size

WEB EXTRA

Go to www.FonsandPorter.com/unpsizes to download *Quilt Top Assembly Diagrams* for these size options.

Quilting Diagram

TRIED & TRUE

Use nine blocks to make a Christmas table topper.
Fabrics shown here are from the Peppermint & Hollyberries
collection by Nancy Halvorsen for Benartex. ✳

QUILT DESIGNED BY **Emily and Rachel Sheeder**.
MADE BY **Mary Ocker**. MACHINE QUILTED BY **Jean Nolte**.

Rachel's Sunset

This bright medallion-style quilt makes a perfect snuggler for TV time or a topper for a big-girl bed.

PROJECT RATING: EASY

Size: 54" × 66"

MATERIALS

¾ yard light yellow print
⅞ yard dark yellow print
½ yard light orange print
1 yard dark orange print
¾ yard very light pink print
½ yard light pink print
½ yard medium pink print
1⅜ yards dark pink print
½ yard light pink plaid
⅜ yard medium pink plaid
⅝ yard dark pink stripe
Paper-backed fusible web
3½ yards backing fabric
Twin-size quilt batting

Cutting

Measurements include ¼" seam allowances. Daisy pattern is on page 49. Follow manufacturer's instructions for using fusible web.

From light yellow print, cut:

- 1 (7¼") square. Cut square in half diagonally in both directions to make 4 quarter-square B triangles (2 are extra).
- 2 (6⅞"-wide) strips. From strips, cut 10 (6⅞") squares. Cut squares in half diagonally to make 20 half-square A triangles.
- 4 Daisies.
- 5 Daisy Centers.

From dark yellow print, cut:

- 1 (7¼") square. Cut square in half diagonally in both directions to make 4 quarter-square B triangles.
- 3 (6⅞"-wide) strips. From strips, cut 12 (6⅞") squares. Cut squares in half diagonally to make 24 half-square A triangles.

From light orange print, cut:

- 2 (6⅞"-wide) strips. From strips, cut 8 (6⅞") squares. Cut squares in half diagonally to make 16 half-square A triangles.

From dark orange print, cut:
- 1 (7¼") square. Cut square in half diagonally in both directions to make 4 quarter-square B triangles (2 are extra).
- 3 (6⅞"-wide) strips. From strips, cut 11 (6⅞") squares. Cut squares in half diagonally to make 22 half-square A triangles.
- 5 Daisies.
- 4 Daisy Centers.

From very light pink print, cut:
- 1 (7¼"-wide) strip. From strip, cut 2 (7¼") squares. Cut squares in half diagonally in both directions to make 8 quarter-square B triangles.
- 2 (6⅞"-wide) strips. From strips, cut 10 (6⅞") squares. Cut squares in half diagonally to make 20 half-square A triangles.
- 1 (3⅞"-wide) strip. From strip, cut 2 (3⅞") squares. Cut squares in half diagonally to make 4 half-square C triangles.

From light pink print, cut:
- 1 (7¼") square. Cut square in half diagonally in both directions to make 4 quarter-square B triangles.
- 1 (6⅞"-wide) strip. From strip, cut 4 (6⅞") squares. Cut squares in half diagonally to make 8 half-square A triangles.

From medium pink print, cut:
- 2 (6⅞"-wide) strips. From strips, cut 6 (6⅞") squares. Cut squares in half diagonally to make 12 half-square A triangles.

From dark pink print, cut:
- 1 (7¼") square. Cut square in half diagonally in both directions to make 4 quarter-square B triangles.
- 2 (6⅞"-wide) strips. From strips, cut 8 (6⅞") squares. Cut squares in half diagonally to make 16 half-square A triangles.

- 2 (3⅞"-wide) strips. From strips, cut 16 (3⅞") squares. Cut squares in half diagonally to make 32 half-square C triangles.
- 7 (2¼"-wide) strips for binding.

From light pink plaid, cut:
- 2 (6⅞"-wide) strips. From strips, cut 8 (6⅞") squares. Cut squares in half diagonally to make 16 half-square A triangles.

From medium pink plaid, cut:
- 2 (4¾"-wide) strips. From strips, cut 9 (4¾") D squares.

From dark pink stripe, cut:
- 1 (7¼") square. Cut square in half diagonally in both directions to make 4 quarter-square B triangles.
- 2 (6⅞"-wide) strips. From strips, cut 6 (6⅞") squares. Cut squares in half diagonally to make 12 half-square A triangles.

Unit Assembly

1. Join 1 dark orange A triangle and 1 light yellow A triangle as shown in *Unit 1 Diagrams*. Make 20 dark orange/light yellow Unit 1.

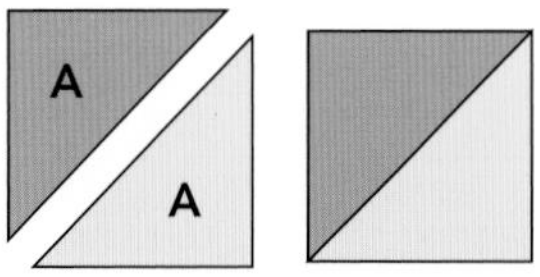

Unit 1 Diagrams

2. In the same manner, make 20 dark yellow/very light pink, 12 dark pink/medium pink, 16 light pink plaid/light orange, and 8 dark pink stripe/light pink Unit 1.

3. Join 1 dark orange B triangle, 1 light yellow B triangle, and 1 dark orange A triangle as shown in *Unit 2 Diagrams*. Make 2 dark orange/light yellow Unit 2.

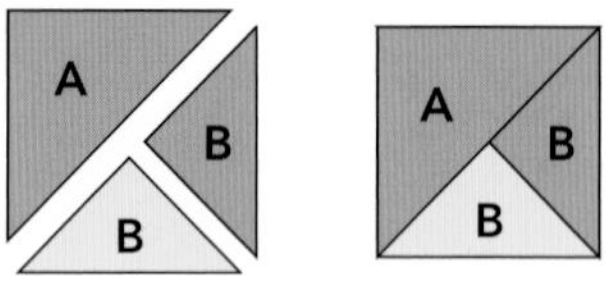

Unit 2 Diagrams

4. In the same manner, make 4 dark yellow/very light pink, 4 dark pink stripe/light pink, and 4 dark pink/very light pink Unit 2.

5. Join 1 medium pink plaid D square and 4 dark pink C triangles as shown in *Daisy Unit Diagrams*. Make 8 medium pink plaid/dark pink Daisy Unit backgrounds.

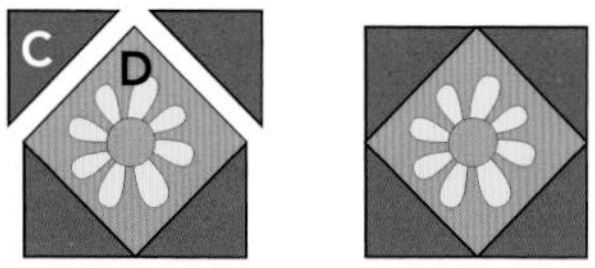

Daisy Unit Diagrams

6. In the same manner, make 1 medium pink plaid/very light pink Daisy Unit background.

7. Arrange 1 Daisy and 1 Daisy Center on Daisy Unit background as shown in *Daisy Unit Diagrams*. Fuse pieces in place. Machine zigzag around pieces using thread colors to match appliqué pieces. Make 5 Daisy Units using orange daisies with yellow centers and 4 Daisy Units using yellow daisies with orange centers.

Sew **Smart**™

To prevent a shadow through yellow pieces which overlap darker colors, line the appliqué pieces with white fabric. —Liz

Quilt Top Assembly Diagram

This quilt is so easy and fun to make,
you'll want to make two! *

Quilt Assembly

1. Lay out units as shown in *Quilt Top Assembly Diagram*.

2. Join into rows; join rows to complete quilt top.

Finishing

1. Divide backing into 2 (1¾-yard) pieces. Join pieces lengthwise. Seam will run horizontally.

2. Layer backing, batting, and quilt top; baste. Quilt as desired. Quilt shown was outline quilted around the daisies and with an overall daisy and leaf design *(Quilting Diagram)*.

3. Join 2¼"-wide dark pink strips into 1 continuous piece for straight-grain French-fold binding. Add binding to quilt.

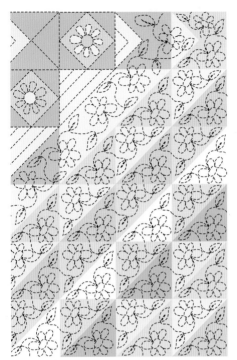

Quilting Diagram

Patterns are shown full size for use with fusible web. Add ³/₁₆" seam allowance for hand appliqué.

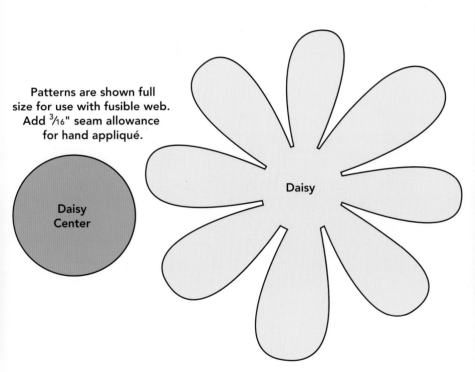

Daisy Center

Daisy

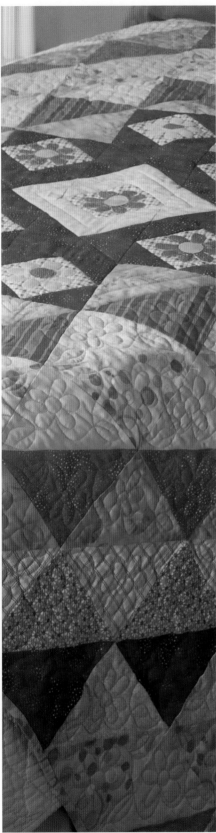

QUILT DESIGNED BY **Dodi Lee Poulsen**.

MADE BY **Dodi Lee Poulsen and Heidi Fisher**. MACHINE QUILTED BY **Valerie Woods**.

Tiny Treasures

Create a treasured quilt for a child's bed or wall using this design by Dodi Lee Poulsen. Try hand appliqué using our easy techniques in *Sew Easy: Interfacing Appliqué* on page 57.

PROJECT RATING: INTERMEDIATE

Size: 48" × 48"

MATERIALS

1½ yards yellow polka-dot for center and corner block background

½ yard white print

¾ yard light pink print

1 fat eighth★ medium pink polka-dot

½ yard dark pink print

4" square dark pink polka-dot

⅝ yard pink plaid

1⅛ yard green polka-dot

Paper-backed fusible web or lightweight, non-fusible interfacing

3 yards backing fabric

Twin-size quilt batting

★fat eighth = 9" × 20"

Cutting

Measurements include ¼" seam allowances. Patterns for Fan Blade, Fan Center and appliqué pieces are on page 56. Follow manufacturer's instructions if using fusible web. Instructions for easy interfacing appliqué are in *Sew Easy: Interfacing Appliqué* on page 57.

From yellow polka-dot, cut:

• 1 (17"-wide) strip. From strip, cut 1 (17") center square and 1 (12½") H square.

• 1 (12½"-wide) strip. From strip, cut 3 (12½") H squares.

• 6 (2¼"-wide) strips for binding.

• 2 (1¾"-wide) strips. From strips, cut 4 (1¾" × 19") E rectangles.

• 3 A circles.

From white print, cut:

• 12 Fan Blades.

• 2 (1¾"-wide) strips. From strips, cut 4 (1¾" × 19") E rectangles.

• 15 Small Flower Petals.

From light pink print, cut:

- 3 (6½"-wide) strips. From strips, cut 32 (6½" × 3½") G rectangles.
- 2 (1¾"-wide) strips. From strips, cut 4 (1¾" × 19") E rectangles.
- 15 Small Flower Petals.

From medium pink polka-dot, cut:

- 5 Large Flower Petals.
- 4 Fan Centers.

From dark pink print, cut:

- 3 (3½"-wide) strips. From strips, cut 32 (3½") F squares.
- 2 (1¾"-wide) strips. From strips, cut 2 (1¾" × 19") E rectangles and 2 (1¾" × 16½") D rectangles.
- 3 A circles.

From dark pink polka-dot, cut:

- 3 B circles.

From pink plaid, cut:

- 3 (6½"-wide) strips. From strips, cut 32 (6½" × 3½") G rectangles.
- 1 C circle.

From green polka-dot, cut:

- 2 (5"-wide) strips. From strips, cut 4 (5" × 19") I rectangles.
- 6 (3½"-wide) strips. From strips, cut 64 (3½") F squares.
- 8 Fan Blades.
- 2 Leaves.
- 2 Leaves reversed.
- 1 B circle.

Center Block Assembly

NOTE: Refer to *Sew Easy: Interfacing Appliqué* on page 57 for easy hand appliqué techniques.

1. Position appliqué pieces atop 17" yellow polka-dot center square as shown in *Center Block Diagram*. Machine appliqué pieces to background. Trim block to 16½" square.

Center Block Diagram

2. Referring to *Center Assembly Diagrams*, add dark pink print D rectangles to top and bottom of center block. Add dark pink print E rectangles to sides of block.

3. Join 1 white print E rectangle, 1 yellow polka-dot E rectangle, 1 light pink print E rectangle, and 1 green polka dot I rectangle as shown in *Corner Unit Diagram*. Make 4 Corner Units.

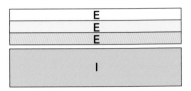

Corner Unit Diagram

4. Add corner units to quilt center as shown in *Center Assembly Diagrams*. Trim center to 24½" square.

Pinwheel Block Assembly

1. Referring to *Flying Geese Unit Diagrams* on page 53, place 1 green polka-dot F square atop 1 pink plaid G rectangle, right sides facing. Stitch diagonally from corner to corner as shown. Trim ¼" beyond stitching. Press open to reveal triangle. Repeat for opposite corner to complete 1 Flying Geese Unit. Make 32 Flying Geese Units.

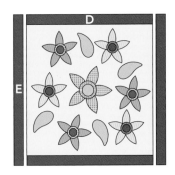

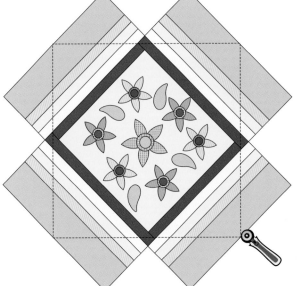

Center Assembly Diagrams

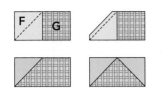

Flying Geese Unit Diagrams

2. Referring to *Pinwheel Unit Diagrams,* place 1 dark pink print F square atop 1 light pink print G rectangle, right sides facing. Stitch diagonally from corner to corner. Trim ¼" beyond stitching. Press open to reveal triangle to complete 1 Pinwheel Unit. Make 32 Pinwheel Units.

Pinwheel Unit Diagrams

3. Lay out 4 Pinwheel Units and 4 Flying Geese Units as shown in *Pinwheel Block Assembly Diagram.* Join units to complete 1 Pinwheel block *(Pinwheel Block Diagram).* Make 8 Pinwheel blocks.

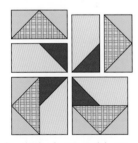

Pinwheel Block Assembly Diagram

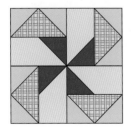

Pinwheel Block Diagram

Fan Block Assembly

1. Referring to *Fan Unit Diagram,* join 3 white print fan blades and 2 green polka dot fan blades, stopping at dot and backstitching. Press seams open.

Fan Unit Diagram

2. Referring to *Fan Block Diagram,* place Fan Unit atop yellow polka-dot H square, aligning edges. Turn under top edges and appliqué Fan Unit to square. Turn under curved edge of medium pink polka dot Fan Center and appliqué atop Fan Unit to complete 1 Fan block. Make 4 Fan blocks.

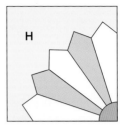

Fan Block Diagram

Quilt Assembly

1. Lay out Center, Pinwheel blocks, and Fan blocks as shown in *Quilt Top Assembly Diagram.* Join into rows; join rows to complete quilt top.

Finishing

1. Divide backing into 2 (1½-yard) lengths. Cut 1 piece in half lengthwise to make 2 narrow panels. Join 1 narrow panel to wider panel. Remaining panel is extra and can be used to make a hanging sleeve.

Quilt Top Assembly Diagram

2. Layer backing, batting, and quilt top; baste. Quilt as desired. Quilt shown was quilted with flowers, leaves, scallops, and swirls *(Quilting Diagram).*

3. Join 2¼"-wide yellow polka dot strips into 1 continuous piece for straight-grain French-fold binding. Add binding to quilt.

WEB EXTRA

To download instructions for pillow and wallhanging shown in photo below visit our Web site at www.FonsandPorter.com/tinyextra.

Quilting Diagram

DESIGNERS

Sisters Dodi Lee Poulsen and Heidi Fisher have been creative since they were small girls, and are passionate about quilting. Together they launched their company, Two Sisters at Squirrel Hollow, named for Heidi's property in the woods of Missouri. Dodi and Heidi teach and lecture individually and together throughout the country. ✳

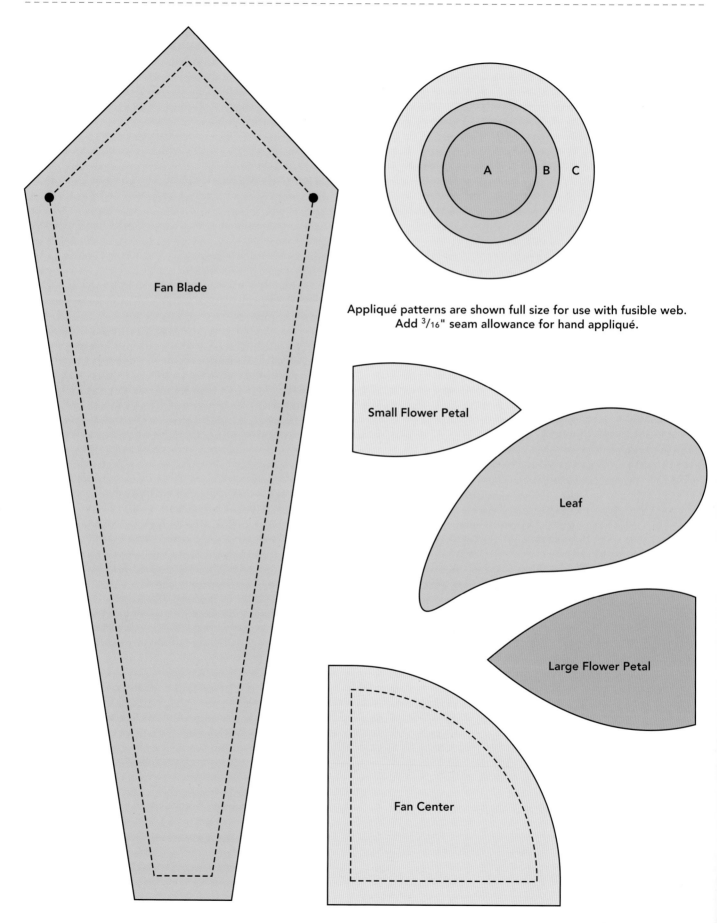

Fan Blade

A B C

Appliqué patterns are shown full size for use with fusible web.
Add $^3/_{16}$" seam allowance for hand appliqué.

Small Flower Petal

Leaf

Large Flower Petal

Fan Center

Interfacing Appliqué

Try this technique to prepare shapes for hand or machine appliqué.

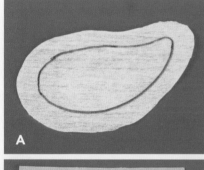

A

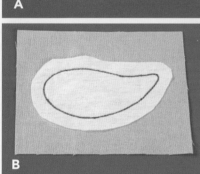

B

C

1. Trace appliqué shape onto lightweight, non-fusible interfacing; cut out about ½" outside of drawn line (*Photo A*).
2. Position interfacing atop right side of fabric. Stitch on drawn line through both layers (*Photo B*).
3. Trim away excess fabric and interfacing, leaving a ⅛" seam allowance. Cut a slit in interfacing to turn appliqué piece (*Photo C*).
4. Turn piece right side out, press shape flat (*Photo D*).
5. Baste pieces to background fabric and appliqué by hand or machine (*Photo E*).

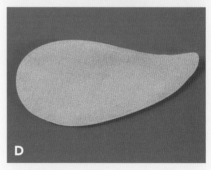

D

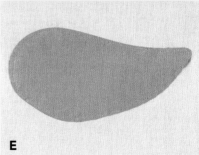

E

Sew **Smart**™

For curved pieces, clip curves or trim seam allowance with pinking shears to make the piece lie flat when it is turned right side out. —Marianne

Anna Lena

It's fun to dress up pre-printed fabric! Pretty little dresses become more stylish with lace, rickrack, buttons, and beads.

PROJECT RATING: INTERMEDIATE
Size: 37½" × 45½"
Blocks: 4 (5¼") Ohio Star blocks

MATERIALS

1 yard dress block print
½ yard pink print for sashing and inner border
½ yard blue print for outer border and binding
1 fat quarter★ white solid for blocks
9 fat quarters★ assorted prints in yellow, pink, blue, and white for blocks and outer border
3¾ yards red medium rickrack
Assorted tiny rickrack, buttons, beads, ribbon, and lace trims for embellishments
Fons & Porter Quarter Inch Seam Marker (optional)
1½ yards backing fabric
Crib-size quilt batting
★fat quarter = 18" × 20"

Cutting

Measurements include ¼" seam allowances. Border strips are exact length needed. You may want to make them longer to allow for piecing variations.

From dress block print, cut:
- 12 (7½") squares, centering 1 dress block in each.

From pink print, cut:
- 6 (2"-wide) strips. From strips, cut 2 (2" × 33") side inner borders and 17 (2" × 7½") A rectangles.
- 2 (1¾"-wide) strips. From strips, cut 2 (1¾" × 27½") top and bottom inner borders.

From blue print, cut:
- 5 (2¼"-wide) strips for binding.
- 3 (1½"-wide) strips. From strips, cut 14 (1½" × 5¾") D rectangles.

From white solid fat quarter, cut:
- 1 (3"-wide) strip. From strip, cut 4 (3") E squares.
- 2 (2¼"-wide) strips. From strips, cut 16 (2¼") C squares.

From 1 yellow print fat quarter, cut:
- 1 (2¼"-wide) strip. From strip, cut 4 (2¼") C squares.
- 1 (2"-wide) strip. From strip, cut 6 (2") B squares.
- 5 (1½"-wide) strips. From strips, cut 14 (1½" × 5¾") D rectangles.

From 1 blue print fat quarter, cut:
- 2 (3"-wide) strips. From strips, cut 8 (3") E squares.
- 5 (1½"-wide) strips. From strips, cut 14 (1½" × 5¾") D rectangles.

From 1 pink print fat quarter, cut:
- 1 (3"-wide) strip. From strips, cut 4 (3") E squares.
- 5 (1½"-wide) strips. From strips, cut 14 (1½" × 5¾") D rectangles.

From remaining fat quarters, cut a total of:
- 23 (1½"-wide) strips. From strips, cut 68 (1½" × 5¾") D rectangles.

Dress Block Assembly

1. Referring to photo on page 58, embellish dress blocks as desired. We used tiny rickrack, ¼"-diameter buttons, and scraps of lace, ribbon, and crocheted trims.

> ### Sew **Smart**™
> To make apron skirt, cut a white solid 2½" × 5" rectangle. Make a narrow hem on bottom and side edges. Gather top edge, and insert under ⅜"-wide finished band. — Marianne

2. Topstitch embellishments in place.

Block Assembly

1. Referring to *Sew Easy: Quick Hourglass Units* on page 61, make 16 Hourglass Units using blue print, pink print, and white solid E squares.

2. Lay out 4 Hourglass Units, 4 white solid C squares, and 1 yellow print C square as shown in *Block Assembly Diagram*. Join into rows; join rows to complete 1 Ohio Star block *(Block Diagram)*. Make 4 Ohio Star blocks.

Block Assembly Diagram

Block Diagram

Border Assembly

1. Lay out 35 assorted D rectangles as shown in *Quilt Top Assembly Diagram*. Join rectangles to make 1 side outer border. Make 2 side outer borders.

2. In the same manner, make top outer border using 27 D rectangles. Repeat for bottom outer border.

Quilt Assembly

1. Lay out Dress blocks, pink print A rectangles, and yellow print B squares as shown in *Quilt Top Assembly Diagram*. Join into rows; join rows to complete quilt center.

2. Add pink print side inner borders to quilt center.

3. Add pink print top and bottom inner borders to quilt.

4. Add side outer borders to quilt.

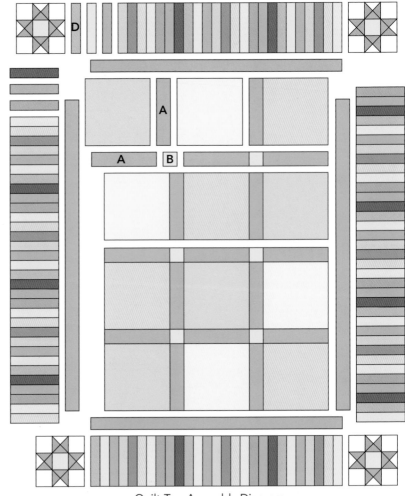

Quilt Top Assembly Diagram

5. Add 1 Ohio Star block to each end of top and bottom outer borders. Add borders to quilt.

Finishing

1. Layer backing, batting, and quilt top; baste. Quilt as desired. Quilt shown was quilted in the ditch, and outline quilted in the dress blocks *(Quilting Diagram)*.

2. Referring to photo on page 58, stitch rickrack on quilt, covering inner border seams as shown.

3. Join 2¼"-wide blue print strips into 1 continuous piece for straight-grain French-fold binding. Add binding to quilt. ✳

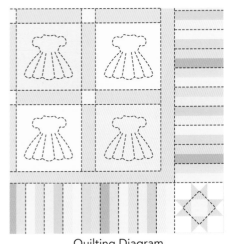

Quilting Diagram

Quick Hourglass Units

Try our quick and easy method to make Hourglass Units without cutting triangles. The Fons & Porter Quarter Inch Seam Marker helps you draw stitching lines quickly.

A

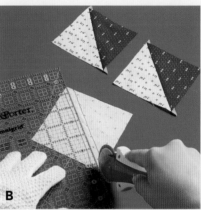

B

1. From 1 light and 1 dark fabric, cut 1 square 1¼" larger than the desired finished size of the Hourglass Unit. For example, to make an Hourglass Unit that will finish 1¾" for *Anna Lena* on page 58, cut 3" squares.

2. On wrong side of light square, place Quarter Inch Seam Marker diagonally across square, with yellow center line positioned exactly at corners. Mark stitching guidelines along both sides of Quarter Inch Seam Marker (*Photo A*). **NOTE:** If you are not using the Fons & Porter Quarter Inch Seam Marker, draw a diagonal line from corner to corner across square. Then draw sewing lines on each side of the first line, ¼" away.

3. Place light square atop dark square, right sides facing; stitch along marked sewing lines.

4. Cut between rows of stitching to make two triangle-squares (*Photo B*). Press seams toward darker fabric.

5. On wrong side of one triangle-square, place Quarter Inch Seam Marker diagonally across square, perpendicular to seam, aligning yellow center line with corners of square. Mark stitching guidelines along both sides of Quarter Inch Seam Marker (*Photo C*). See note in #2 if you are not using the Fons & Porter Quarter Inch Seam Marker.

6. Place triangle-square with drawn line atop matching triangle-square, right sides facing and opposite fabrics facing. Stitch along both drawn lines. Cut between rows of stitching to create 2 Hourglass Units (*Photo D*). Press seam allowances to 1 side. **NOTE:** For Anna Lena, use 1 blue/white triangle-square and 1 blue/pink triangle-square to make 2 Hourglass Units.

C

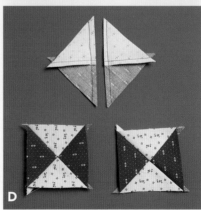

D

Fairies

Sunny yellow and spring green florals surround delicate fairies
in this easy quilt. The fairy blocks and center are cut from fabric panels,
making this a quick project you can finish in no time.

PROJECT RATING: EASY

Size: 66" × 90"

MATERIALS

¾ yard Sunny Sunshine panel for
quilt center

1 yard Sunny Sunshine Fairies panel
for blocks (or enough to cut 18
(6" × 8½") rectangles

1½ yards peach print for sashing
and inner border

2 yards yellow print for outer
border

1¼ yards green print for middle
border and binding

5½ yards backing fabric

Full-size quilt batting

Cutting

Measurements include ¼" seam
allowances. Border strips are exact
length needed. You may want to make
them longer to allow for piecing
variations.

From Sunny Sunshine panel, cut:

• 1 (22½" × 41½") rectangle, centering
design.

**From Sunny Sunshine Fairies panel
fabric, cut:**

• 18 (6" × 8½") Fairy rectangles,
centering design in each.

From peach print, cut:

• 10 (3¾"-wide) strips. From 6 strips,
cut 2 (3¾" × 41½") C sashing
rectangles, 2 (3¾" × 40") D sashing
rectangles, and 2 (3¾" × 40")
top and bottom inner borders.
Piece remaining strips to make
2 (3¾" × 70½") side inner borders.

• 3 (3½"-wide) strips. From strips, cut 8
(3½" × 8½") A sashing rectangles and
6 (3½" × 6") B sashing rectangles.

From yellow print, cut:

• 8 (8½"-wide) strips. Piece strips to
make 2 (8½" × 74½") side outer
borders and 2 (8½" × 66½") top and
bottom outer borders.

From green print, cut:

• 7 (2½"-wide) strips. Piece strips to
make 2 (2½" × 70½") side middle
borders and 2 (2½" × 50½") top and
bottom middle borders.

• 9 (2¼"-wide) strips for binding.

Quilt Assembly

1. Join 5 Fairy rectangles and 4 peach
print A rectangles as shown in *Top
Row Diagram* on page 64. Repeat for
bottom row.

2. Join 4 Fairy rectangles and 3 peach
print B rectangles as shown in *Side
Row Diagram* on page 64. Make 2
side rows.

3. Add C sashing rectangles and side
rows to center panel as shown in
Quilt Top Assembly Diagram on page 64.

4. Add D sashing rectangles and top and
bottom Fairy rows to complete quilt
center.

5. Add peach print top and bottom
inner borders to quilt center. Add side
inner borders to quilt.

6. Repeat for green print middle borders
and yellow print outer borders.

Finishing

1. Divide backing into 2 (2¾-yard)
lengths. Join panels lengthwise. Cut
1 piece in half lengthwise to make 2
narrow panels. Join 1 narrow panel to
each side of wider panel; press seam
allowances toward narrow panels.

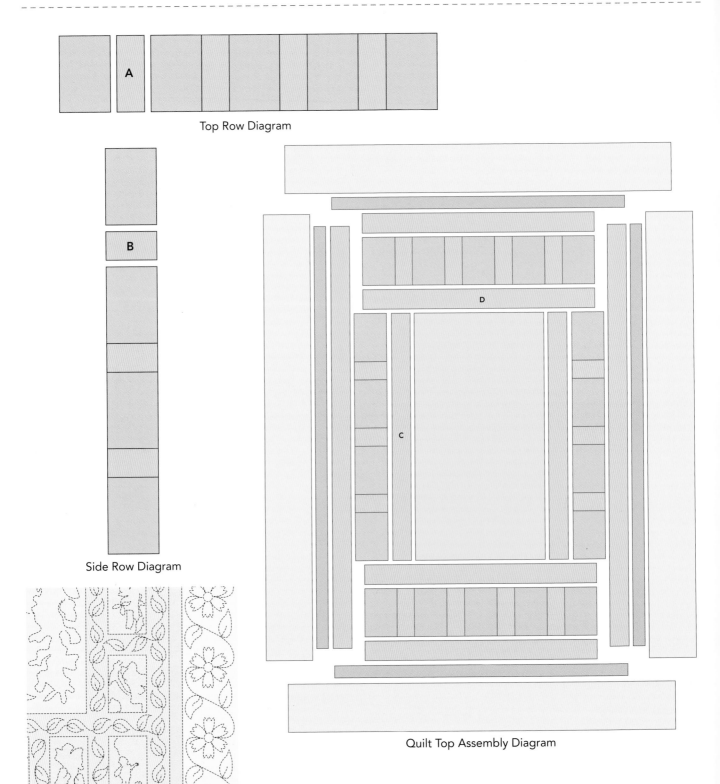

Top Row Diagram

Side Row Diagram

Quilting Diagram

Quilt Top Assembly Diagram

2. Layer backing, batting, and quilt top; baste. Quilt as desired. Quilt shown was quilted in the ditch around blocks and borders, and with leaves in the sashing and a floral design in the border *(Quilting Diagram)*.

3. Join 2¼"-wide green print strips into 1 continuous piece for straight-grain French-fold binding. Add binding to quilt. ✳

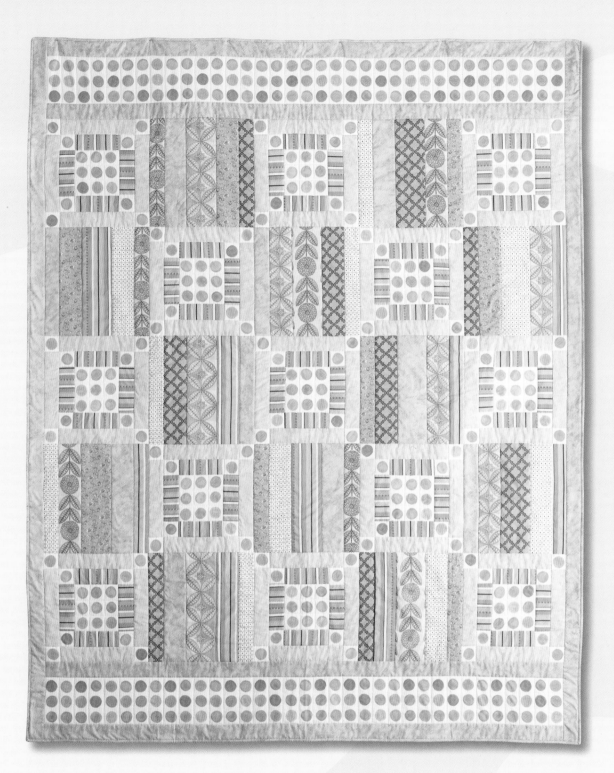

Ocean Breeze

Make a quilt in fun fabrics that are perfect for a teenager.

The blues and greens are fresh as an ocean breeze.

PROJECT RATING: EASY

Size: 74" × 90"

Blocks: 25 (14") blocks

MATERIALS

1½ yards light green print

2 yards aqua print for borders
and binding

1¼ yards green stripe

3½ yards large dot print

NOTE: If not fussy cutting,
2 yards are required.

½ yard each of 5 assorted
light green and aqua stripes and
prints

5½ yards backing fabric

Full-size quilt batting

Cutting

Measurements include ¼" seam
allowances. Border strips are exact
length needed. You may want to make
them longer to allow for piecing
variations.

From light green print, cut:

• 4 (10½"-wide) strips. From strips,
cut 52 (10½" × 2½") D rectangles.

From aqua print, cut:

• 1 (14½"-wide) strip. From strip,
cut 2 (14½" × 4½") G rectangles,
4 (14½" × 3½") F rectangles, and
4 (14½" × 2½") E rectangles.

• 13 (2½"-wide) strips. Piece strips to
make 4 (2½" × 70½") top and bottom
borders and 2 (2½" × 90½") side
borders.

• 9 (2¼"-wide) strips for binding.

From green stripe, cut:

• 9 (2½"-wide) strips. From strips,
cut 52 (2½" × 6½") C rectangles.

• 1 (14½"-wide) strip. From strip,
cut 2 (14½" × 4½") G rectangles,
4 (14½" × 3½") F rectangles, and
4 (14½" × 2½") E rectangles.

From large dot print, cut:

• 11 (2½"-wide) strips, centering dots
on each. From strips, cut
104 (2½") B squares.

From remainder of large dot print, cut:

• 3 (6½"-wide) **lengthwise** strips,
centering dots on each. From strips,
cut 2 (6½" × 70½") strips for top
and bottom borders and 13 (6½") A
squares, centering dots on each.

**From each assorted print or stripe,
cut:**

• 1 (14½"-wide) strip. From strips, cut a
total of 8 (14½" × 4½") G rectangles,
16 (14½" × 3½") F rectangles, and 16
(14½" × 2½") E rectangles.

Block Assembly

1. Lay out 1 A square, 8 B squares, 4
green stripe C rectangles, and 4 light
green print D rectangles as shown
in *Block 1 Assembly Diagram*. Join
to complete 1 Block 1 (*Block 1
Diagram*). Make 13 Block 1.

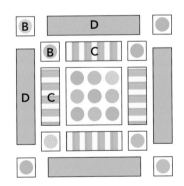

Block 1 Assembly Diagram

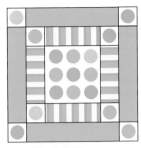

Block 1 Diagram

2. Lay out 2 assorted E rectangles,
2 assorted F rectangles, and 1 G
rectangle as shown in *Block 2
Assembly Diagram*. Join to complete 1
Block 2 (*Block 2 Diagram*). Make 12
Block 2.

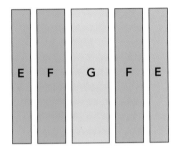

Block 2 Assembly Diagram

Block 2 Diagram

Quilt Assembly

1. Lay out blocks as shown in *Quilt Top
Assembly Diagram*. Join into rows;
join rows to complete quilt center.

2. Join 2 aqua print top and bottom
borders and 1 large dot border to
make top border. Repeat for bottom
border.

3. Add top and bottom borders to quilt
center.

4. Add aqua print side borders to quilt.

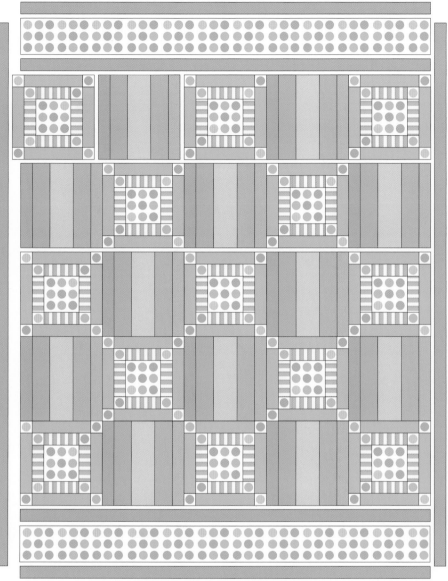

Quilt Top Assembly Diagram

Finishing

1. Divide backing into 2 (2¾-yard) lengths. Cut 1 piece in half lengthwise to make 2 narrow panels. Join 1 narrow panel to each side of wider panel; press seam allowances toward narrow panels.

2. Layer backing, batting, and quilt top; baste. Quilt as desired. Quilt shown was quilted in the ditch and with straight lines between rows of dots in the blocks and border *(Quilting Diagram)*.

3. Join 2¼"-wide aqua print strips into 1 continuous piece for straight-grain French-fold binding. Add binding to quilt.

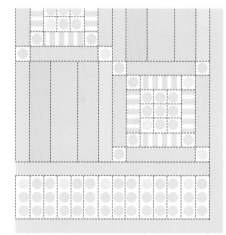

Quilting Diagram

TRIED & TRUE

We made this dramatic table runner using vibrant prints from the Arabella collection by Pat Sloan for P&B Textiles.

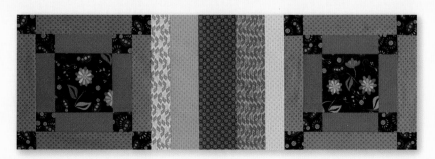

Anna's Album

A traditional Album block takes on a trendy new look in warm,
natural colors. Check your stash or the local quilt shop for a large-scale, upbeat
print to use for the border.

PROJECT RATING: INTERMEDIATE

Size: 54" × 67½"

Blocks: 12 (12") Album blocks

MATERIALS

6 fat quarters★ assorted prints
in tangerine, coral, cocoa, and
chocolate for blocks

⅝ yard each of 2 light peach prints
for block backgrounds

¾ yard peach print for sashing

⅜ yard brown print for inner
border

1⅛ yards pink floral print for outer
border

½ yard pink stripe for binding

Twin-size quilt batting

3¼ yards backing fabric

Fons & Porter Triangle Trimmers
(optional)

★fat quarter = 18" × 20"

Cutting

Measurements include ¼" seam allowances. Border strips are exact length
needed. You may want to make them
longer to allow for piecing variations.

From each fat quarter, cut:

• 6 (2⅝"-wide) strips. From strips,
cut 4 (2⅝" × 6⅞") C rectangles,
12 (2⅝" × 4¾") B rectangles, and
4 (2⅝") A squares.

From each light peach print, cut:

• 2 (4¼"-wide) strips. From strips, cut
18 (4¼") squares. Cut squares in half
diagonally in both directions to make
72 quarter-square D triangles.

• 3 (2⅝"-wide) strips. From strips,
cut 6 (2⅝" × 6⅞") C rectangles and
12 (2⅝") A squares.

• 1 (2⅜"-wide) strip. From strip, cut
12 (2⅜") squares. Cut squares in half
diagonally to make 24 half-square E
triangles.

From peach print, cut:

• 12 (2"-wide) strips. From strips,
cut 16 (2" × 12½") vertical sashing
strips. Piece remaining strips to make
5 (2" × 42½") horizontal sashing strips.

From brown print, cut:

• 6 (1½"-wide) strips. Piece strips
to make 2 (1½" × 56") side inner
borders and 2 (1½" × 44½") top and
bottom inner borders.

From pink floral print, cut:

• 6 (5½"-wide) strips. Piece strips
to make 2 (5½" × 58") side outer
borders and 2 (5½" × 54½") top and
bottom outer borders.

From pink stripe, cut:

• 7 (2¼"-wide) strips for binding.

Block Assembly

> ### Sew **Smart**™
>
> To make quick work of assembling
> Album blocks, trim the points
> on the D and E triangles using
> Fons & Porter Triangle Trimmers.
> —Marianne

1. Referring to *Block Assembly Diagram*,
lay out 1 matching set of 2 A squares,
6 B rectangles, and 2 C rectangles;
and 1 matching set of 2 light peach A
squares, 1 C rectangle, 12 D triangles,
and 4 E triangles as shown in *Block
Assembly Diagram* on page 70. Join
pieces in diagonal rows; join rows
to complete 1 Album block (*Block
Diagram*).

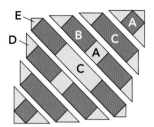

Block Assembly Diagram

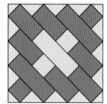

Block Diagram

2. Make 12 Album blocks.

Quilt Assembly

1. Lay out blocks and sashing strips as shown in *Quilt Top Assembly Diagram*. Join into rows; join rows to complete quilt center.

2. Add brown print side inner borders to quilt center. Add top and bottom inner borders to quilt.

3. Repeat for pink floral print outer borders.

Finishing

1. Divide backing into 2 (1⅝-yard) lengths. Join pieces lengthwise. Seam will run horizontally.

2. Layer backing, batting, and quilt top; baste. Quilt as desired. Quilt shown was quilted with a feather design in the blocks and an allover design in the block backgrounds, sashing, and outer border *(Quilting Diagram)*.

3. Join 2¼"-wide pink stripe strips into 1 continuous piece for straight-grain French-fold binding. Add binding to quilt.

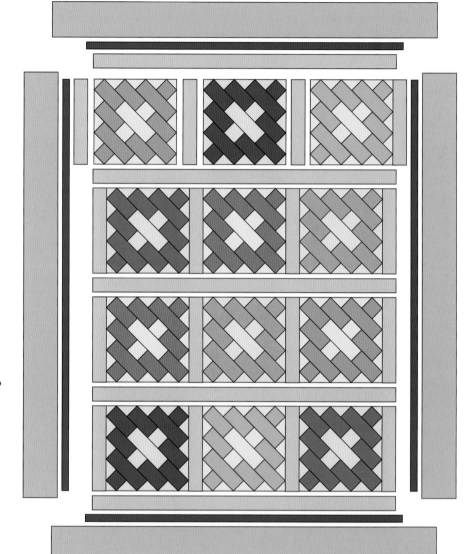

Quilt Top Assembly Diagram

Quilting Diagram

SIZE OPTIONS

	Twin (67½" × 81")	Full (81" × 94½")	Queen (94½" × 94½")
Blocks	20	30	36
Setting	4 × 5 blocks	5 × 6 blocks	6 × 6 blocks

MATERIALS

Assorted prints	10 fat quarters	15 fat quarters	18 fat quarters
2 Light Peach prints	1⅛ yards each	1⅜ yards each	1½ yards each
Peach print	1¼ yards	1½ yards	1¾ yards
Coco print	⅜ yard	⅝ yard	¾ yard
Pink Floral print	1⅜ yards	1½ yards	1¾ yards
Binding	¾ yard	¾ yard	⅞ yard
Backing Fabric	5 yards	7¼ yards	8½ yards
Batting	Twin-size	Queen-size	King-size

WEB EXTRA

Go to www.FonsandPorter.com/annasizes to download *Quilt Top Assembly Diagrams* for these size options.

TRIED & TRUE

Make a set of blocks for your own signature quilt. For this version, we used fabrics designed by Robbi Joy Eklow for Quilting Treasures.

DESIGNER

Jean Ann Wright has been designing quilts for many years. Her favorites are made from traditional blocks laid out in new ways. Jean Ann says she never runs out of ideas! ✳

Completing a Signature Quilt

Completing a signature quilt to commemorate an important event in someone's life takes careful organization. Begin early enough so you can get all of the signatures and still have time to finish the quilt by your deadline. Allow about 12 weeks for the project from start to finish (longer if you will be hand quilting). Use our tips and timeline to make your project a success.

Tips

- Choose a patchwork block that has an area large enough for signatures. Find a block that has a patchwork area you can construct while you you are waiting for signature pieces to be returned.
- Plan to leave the signature areas on some blocks blank to be signed later.
- Select a light-colored fabric for the signature area so writing will show.

Timeline

Week 1
- Plan your quilt design.
- Buy fabric and fabric marking pens to send with signature pieces.
- If you don't plan to quilt the project yourself, schedule an appointment with a machine quilter.

Week 2
- Cut freezer paper pieces the finished size of signature patches. (For *Anna's Album*, cut 2⅛" × 6⅜" rectangles of freezer paper.) Press shiny side of a freezer paper piece to the wrong side of each signature patch to stabilize fabric. Cut enough

signature pieces so each person can have an extra in case he/she makes a mistake.
- Write instructions for signing to include when you send the fabric pieces. Warn people to write only in areas backed by freezer paper.
- List signatures you want; mail prepared fabric, pens, instructions, and stamped return envelopes to those on your list. Include a deadline for returning pieces.

Week 3
- Make other parts of the quilt.

Week 4
- Start calling people to remind them to return their signed pieces.
- Continue sewing other sections.

Weeks 5 & 6
- As signatures arrive, remove freezer paper and heat set signatures by pressing with a hot, dry iron.
- Assemble blocks.

Weeks 7 & 8
- Join blocks to complete quilt top and mark quilting designs.

Week 9 to final week
- Quilt the quilt or deliver it to the machine quilter.
- Make binding and quilt label.

Final week
- Stitch binding to quilt and sew label to back.

Sew **Smart**™

Mail pens in a box or padded envelope to prevent breakage which could damage fabric.

Flowers For Hannah

This quilt in soft colors and flannel fabrics is perfect for any season. We love the wool appliqué—it's easy using felted wool that won't fray.

PROJECT RATING: INTERMEDIATE

Size: 52" × 52"

Blocks: 13 (8") Churn Dash blocks

MATERIALS

13 fat quarters★ assorted dark/medium flannel plaids and checks in green, lavender, mauve, blue, orange, and brown

9 fat quarters★ assorted light flannel plaids and stripes

2 fat quarters★ mauve flannel print for binding

2 fat eighths★★ felted wool in mauve and green for appliqué

3 (6") squares felted wool in light brown, dark green, and dark brown for appliqué

1 (10") square tan wool for appliqué

Paper-backed fusible web

3½ yards backing fabric

Twin-size quilt batting

★fat quarter = 18" × 20"

★★fat eighth = 9" × 20"

Cutting

Measurements include ¼" seam allowances. Border strips are exact length needed. You may want to make them longer to allow for piecing variations. Patterns for appliqué are on page 79. Follow manufacturer's instructions for using fusible web.

From each of 9 dark/medium fat quarters, cut:

• 1 (2⅞"-wide) strip. From strip, cut 2 (2⅞") squares. Cut squares in half diagonally to make 4 half-square A triangles.

• 1 (1½"-wide) strip. From strip, cut 4 (1½"× 4½") B rectangles.

From each of 6 of these same fat quarters, cut:

• 1 (9¼"-wide) strip. From strip, cut 1 (9¼") square. Cut square in half diagonally in both directions to make 4 quarter-square C triangles.

From each remaining dark/medium fat quarter, cut:

• 1 (4½"-wide) strip. From strip, cut 1 (4½") D square and 2 (2⅞") squares.

Cut (2⅞") squares in half diagonally to make 4 half-square A triangles.

• 1 (1½"-wide) strip. From strip, cut 4 (1½" × 4½") B rectangles.

From remainders of dark/medium fat quarters, cut a total of:

• 48 (4½") D squares for outer border.

From each light fat quarter, cut:

• 1 (4½"-wide) strip. From strip, cut 1 (4½") D square and 2 (2⅞") squares. Cut (2⅞") squares in half diagonally to make 4 half-square A triangles.

• 1 (1½"-wide) strip. From strip, cut 4 (1½" × 4½") B rectangles.

From each of 6 light fat quarters, cut:

• 1 (9¼"-wide) strip. From strip, cut 1 (9¼") square. Cut square in half diagonally in both directions to make 4 quarter-square C triangles.

From each of 4 light fat quarters, cut:

• 2 (2⅞") squares. Cut squares in half diagonally to make 4 half-square A triangles.

• 1 (1½"-wide) strip. From strip, cut 4 (1½" × 4½") B rectangles.

From remainders of light fat quarters, cut a total of:

- 11 (2½"-wide) strips. Piece strips to make 2 (2½" × 44½") top and bottom inner borders and 2 (2½" × 40½") side inner borders.

From mauve fat quarters, cut a total of:

- 13 (2½"-wide) strips for binding.

From mauve wool, cut:

- 45 Coneflower Petals.

From green wool, cut:

- 9 Stems.
- 18 Leaves.

From light brown wool, cut:

- 9 Coneflower Centers.

From dark green wool, cut:

- 8 Leaves.

From tan wool, cut:

- 4 Sunflowers.

From dark brown wool, cut:

- 4 Sunflower Centers.

Block Assembly

1. Choose 1 matching set of 4 dark A triangles and 4 B rectangles and 1 matching set of 4 light A triangles, 4 B rectangles, and 1 D square.

2. Join 1 dark A triangle and 1 light A triangle to make a triangle-square *(Triangle-Square Diagrams)*. Make 4 triangle-squares.

Triangle-Square Diagrams

3. Join 1 dark B rectangle and 1 light B rectangle to make a Side Unit *(Side Unit Diagrams)*. Make 4 Side Units.

Side Unit Diagrams

4. Lay out triangle-squares, Side Units, and D square as shown in *Block Assembly Diagram*. Join into rows; join rows to complete 1 light Churn Dash block *(Block Diagram)*. Make 9 light blocks.

Block Assembly Diagram   Block Diagram

5. In the same manner, make 4 dark Churn Dash blocks using dark D squares.

6. Arrange 5 Coneflower Petals, 1 Coneflower Center, 1 Stem, and 2 Leaves on 1 light block background as shown in photo on page 74. Fuse pieces in place. Using matching thread and blanket stitch, appliqué pieces on block background (See

Sew Easy: Blanket Stitch on page 77). Make 9 Coneflower blocks.

7. Arrange 1 Sunflower, 1 Sunflower Center, and 2 Leaves on 1 dark block background as shown in photo on page 74. Fuse pieces in place. Using matching thread and blanket stitch, appliqué pieces on block background. Make 4 Sunflower blocks.

Hourglass Unit Assembly

1. Lay out 2 dark C triangles and 2 light C triangles as shown in *Hourglass Unit Diagrams*. Join triangles to complete 1 Hourglass Unit.

2. Make 12 Hourglass Units.

Hourglass Unit Diagrams

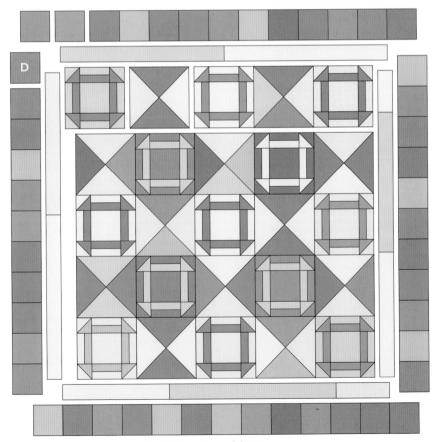

Quilt Top Assembly Diagram

Quilt Assembly

1. Lay out blocks and Hourglass Units as shown in *Quilt Top Assembly Diagram*. Join into rows; join rows to complete quilt center.
2. Add side inner borders to quilt center. Add top and bottom inner borders to quilt.
3. Referring to *Quilt Top Assembly Diagram*; join 11 D squares to make 1 side outer border. Make 2 side outer borders.
4. In the same manner, join 13 D squares to make top outer border. Repeat to make bottom outer border.
5. Add pieced side borders to quilt center. Add pieced top and bottom borders to quilt.

Finishing

1. Divide backing into 2 (1¾-yard) lengths. Cut 1 piece in half lengthwise to make 2 narrow panels. Join 1 narrow panel to wider panel. Remaining panel is extra and can be used to make a hanging sleeve.
2. Layer backing, batting, and quilt top; baste. Quilt as desired. Quilt shown was echo quilted in the blocks and has feather designs in Hourglass units and borders *(Quilting Diagram)*.
3. Join 2½"-wide mauve strips into 1 continuous piece for straight-grain French-fold binding. Add binding to quilt.

Quilting Diagram

Sew Smart™

When making flannel quilts, I like to cut my binding strips 2½" wide.
—Liz

Blanket Stitch

Use this decorative stitch for *Flowers for Hannah*.

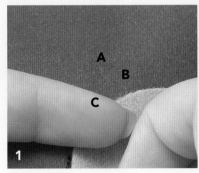

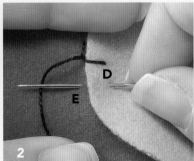

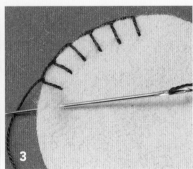

1. Bring needle to right side of fabric at A, just outside the edge of the appliqué piece. Insert needle at B and bring it up at C, over the thread. Pull thread taut so stitch lies flat, but not tight enough to pucker fabric.
2. Insert needle at D and bring it up at E, over the thread.
3. Continue in this manner. Secure last stitch with a tiny stitch to anchor the loop.

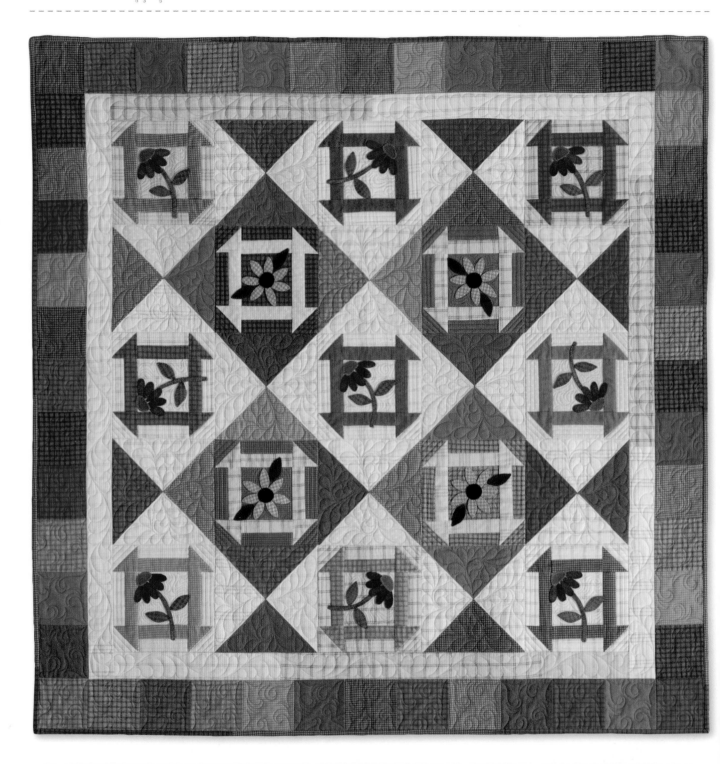

DESIGNER

Paula Stoddard has a passion for quilting and has worked as an independent longarm quilter. She now designs patterns full time for her company, Pacific Patchwork. She enjoys traveling to teach and lecture to quilt guilds and quilt shops.

Patterns are shown full size and are reversed for use with fusible web. Add ³⁄₁₆" seam allowance for hand appliqué.

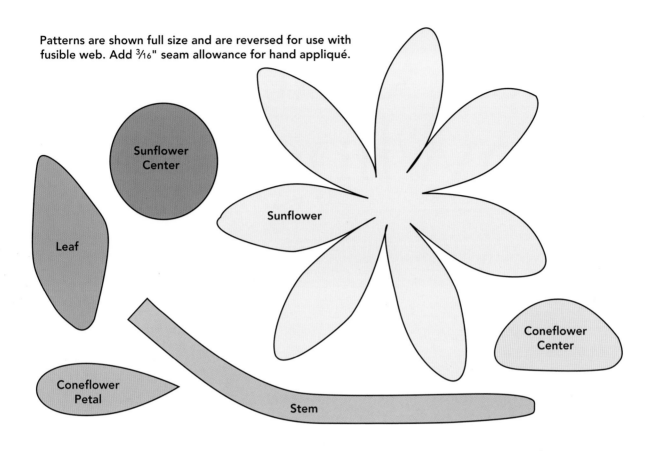

SIZE OPTIONS

	Crib (36" × 36")	Twin (68" × 100")
Blocks	5	39
Hourglass Units	4	38

MATERIALS

	Crib (36" × 36")	Twin (68" × 100")
Dark to Medium Prints	5 fat quarters	39 fat quarters
Light Prints	4 fat quarters	27 fat quarters
Mauve, green, tan wool	1 fat eighth each	½ yard each
Light brown, dark green, dark brown wool	6" square each	1 fat eighth each
Binding Fabric	³⁄₈ yard	¾ yard
Backing Fabric	1¼ yards	6 yards
Batting	Crib-size	Queen-size

 **WEB** EXTRA

Go to www.FonsandPorter.com/hannahsizes to download *Quilt Top Assembly Diagrams* for these size options.

Black Cats Prowling

Virginia Anderson used a pattern designed by Sara Nephew to create this spooky cat quilt that showcases a collection of black prints. To learn how to add piping to your binding as Virginia did, see *Sew Easy: Binding With Piping* on page 85.

PROJECT RATING: INTERMEDIATE

Size: 57" × 69"

Blocks: 19 (9") Cat blocks and 1 (9") Moon block

MATERIALS

19 fat eighths★ assorted black prints for cats

3¼ yards blue print for background

⅜ yard gold print for moon and piping

⅝ yard black print for binding

3½ yards backing fabric

Rug weight acrylic yarn (for piping)

Glue stick (optional)

Twin-size quilt batting

38 (½"-diameter) gold buttons

38 (⅜"-diameter) black buttons

★fat eighth = 9" × 20"

NOTE: The buttons on this quilt may present a choking hazard for small children.

Cutting

Measurements include ¼" seam allowances. Border strips are exact length needed. You may want to make them longer to allow for piecing variations.

From each black print fat eighth, cut:

- 1 (3½"-wide) strip. From strip, cut 1 (3½") A square, 1 (3½" × 5") B rectangle, and 3 (3½" × 2") C rectangles.
- 1 (3⅞") square. Cut square in half diagonally to make 2 half-square D triangles. (1 is extra.)
- 4 (2") E squares.

From blue print, cut:

- 6 (6½"-wide) strips. Piece strips to make 4 (6½" × 57½") border strips.
- 2 (3⅞"-wide) strips. From strips, cut 12 (3⅞") squares. Cut squares in half diagonally to make 24 half-square D triangles (1 is extra).
- 5 (3½"-wide) strips. Piece strips to make 4 (3½" × 45½") horizontal sashing strips.

- 11 (3½"-wide) strips. From strips, cut 16 (3½" × 9½") vertical sashing strips, 19 (3½" × 5") B rectangles, 39 (3½") A squares, and 19 (3½" × 2") C rectangles.
- 2 (2"-wide) strips. From strips, cut 38 (2") E squares.

From gold print, cut:

- 7 (1"-wide) strips for piping.
- 2 (3⅞") squares. Cut squares in half diagonally to make 4 half-square D triangles.
- 1 (3½") A square.

From black print, cut:

- 7 (2½"-wide) strips for binding.

Cat Block Assembly

1. Choose 1 set of black print pieces and 2 A squares, 1 B rectangle, 1 blue print C rectangle, 1 blue print D triangle, and 2 blue print E squares.

2. Referring to *Unit 1 Diagrams*, place 1 black print E square atop 1 blue print C rectangle, right sides facing. Stitch diagonally from corner to corner as shown. Trim ¼" beyond stitching. Press open to reveal triangle. Repeat for opposite end of rectangle to complete Unit 1.

Unit 1 Diagrams

3. Referring to *Unit 2 Diagrams*, place 1 blue print E square atop black print A square, right sides facing. Stitch diagonally from corner to corner as shown. Trim ¼" beyond stitching. Press open to reveal triangle.

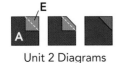

Unit 2 Diagrams

4. Referring to *Unit 3 Diagrams*, place 1 black print E square atop blue print A square, right sides facing. Stitch diagonally from corner to corner as shown. Trim ¼" beyond stitching. Press open to reveal triangle. Repeat for adjacent corner to complete Unit 3.

Unit 3 Diagrams

5. Referring to *Unit 4 Diagrams*, join 1 black print D triangle and 1 blue print D triangle to make a triangle-square. Place 1 blue print E square atop triangle-square, right sides facing. Stitch diagonally from corner to corner as shown. Trim ¼" beyond stitching. Press open to reveal triangle.

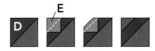

Unit 4 Diagrams

6. Lay out pieces as shown in *Cat Block Assembly Diagram*. Join into segments; join segments to complete 1 Cat block (*Cat Block Diagram*). Make 11 Cat blocks.

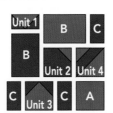

Cat Block Assembly Diagram

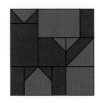

Cat Block Diagram

7. Make 8 reverse Cat blocks as shown in *Reverse Cat Block Diagram*.

Reverse Cat Block Diagram

Moon Block Assembly

1. Join 1 gold print D triangle and 1 blue print D triangle to make a triangle-square. Make 4 triangle-squares.

2. Lay out 4 triangle-squares, 1 blue print A square, 1 gold print A square, and 1 vertical sashing strip as shown in *Moon Block Diagrams*. Join into vertical rows; join rows to complete Moon block.

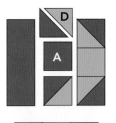

Moon Block Diagrams

Quilt Assembly

1. Lay out Cat blocks, Moon block, vertical sashing strips, and horizontal sashing strips as shown in *Quilt Top Assembly Diagram*. Join into rows; join rows to complete quilt center.

2. Add borders to sides of quilt. Add borders to top and bottom of quilt.

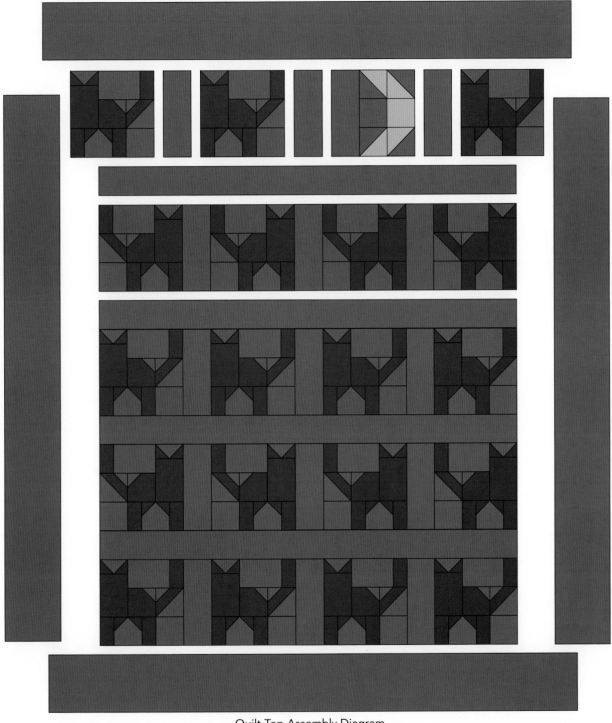

Quilt Top Assembly Diagram

Finishing

1. Divide backing into 2 (1¾-yard) pieces. Join panels lengthwise. Seam will run horizontally.

2. Layer backing, batting, and quilt top; baste. Quilt as desired. Quilt shown was quilted with a diamond grid.

3. Join 2½"-wide black print strips into 1 continuous piece for straight-grain French-fold binding. Join 1"-wide gold strips into 1 continuous piece for piping. Refer to *Sew Easy: Binding with Piping* on page 85 to add binding to quilt.

4. Stack black buttons on gold buttons and sew two sets to each cat for eyes.

DESIGNER

After dabbling in many art forms, Virginia Anderson turned exclusively to quilting when she joined her local guild, Quilters Anonymous, and a small group the same day. She enjoys testing patterns for quilt book authors and making the teapot quilts she designs. Several of her teapot quilts were featured in a special quilt guild exhibit called "Teapot Obsession." ☀

TRIED & TRUE

We made a floral feline with fabric from the Marble Head collection by Ro Gregg for Northcott.

Binding with Piping

Narrow piping inserted along the edge of your binding can be the perfect finish for certain projects. Best of all, you can make and finish this binding completely on the sewing machine.

Supplies

Fabric to make 2½"-wide binding

Fabric to make 1"-wide continuous fabric strip to cover yarn piping filler

Rug-weight acrylic yarn

Zipper foot or piping foot for sewing machine

Clear monofilament nylon thread

Glue Stick

Instructions

1. Begin by measuring around the perimeter of your quilt; add 20" to this measurement to allow for mitering corners of binding and finishing the ends. From binding fabric, make 2½"-wide straight-grain binding this length. From piping cover fabric, make 1"-wide straight-grain strip this length.

2. Insert the yarn in the piping cover strip; loosely baste fabric over yarn piping, using zipper or cording foot (Photo A).

3. To mark the center of the binding strip, fold it in half, wrong sides facing, and press. Open binding back out so it is flat press lightly if desired.

4. Using zipper or cording foot, baste piping to center fold line of binding (Photo B). Fold binding in half with wrong sides facing.

> ### Sew Smart™
> Use a glue stick to "baste" piping to center fold of binding before stitching. —Marianne

5. Trim excess batting and quilt back so ditch between piping and binding will align with first binding stitching when binding is sewn to quilt.

6. Working from the quilt back, align raw edge of binding with raw edge of quilt back. Piping fabric will be on top of binding fabric. Stitch binding to quilt (Photo C). Miter corners and join the ends just as when applying regular binding.

> ### Sew Smart™
> I use my "Liz's Lumpless Binding" technique (General Instructions at the back of this book) to join the ends of the binding. —Liz

7. Bring binding over edge of quilt to front. Use clear monofilament thread (or thread that matches the piping cover fabric) and a zipper or cording foot to topstitch through all layers in the ditch between the piping and the binding (Photo D).

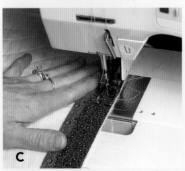

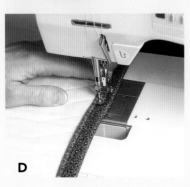

Chillin'

You'll love these super-easy blocks in warm snuggly flannels.
This quilt is so easy and quick—it's great for a last minute gift.

PROJECT RATING: EASY
Size: 50" × 60"

MATERIALS

1¼ yards navy print
1 yard light blue print for border
½ yard medium blue print for blocks
⅜ yard white print for blocks
⅝ yard multicolor stripe for blocks
½ yard dark blue print for binding
3¼ yards backing fabric
Twin-size quilt batting

Cutting

Measurements include ¼" seam allowances. Border strips are exact length needed. You may want to make them longer to allow for piecing variations.

From navy print, cut:
• 4 (10½"-wide) strips. From strips, cut 10 (10½") A squares.

From light blue print, cut:
• 6 (5½"-wide) strips. Piece strips to make 4 (5½" × 50½") borders.

From medium blue print, cut:
• 2 (6½"-wide) strips. From strips, cut 10 (6½") B squares.

From white print, cut:
• 2 (4½"-wide) strips. From strips, cut 10 (4½") C squares.

From multicolor stripe, cut:
• 3 (6½"-wide) strips. From strips, cut 20 (6½" × 4½") D rectangles.

From dark blue print, cut:
• 6 (2½"-wide) strips for binding.

> **Sew Smart™**
> When making flannel quilts, I like to cut my binding strips 2½" wide.
> —Liz

Block Assembly

1. Lay out 1 medium blue B square, 1 white print C square, and 2 stripe D rectangles as shown in *Block Assembly Diagrams.*

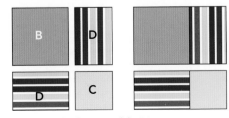

Block Assembly Diagrams

2. Join into rows; join rows to complete 1 block *(Block Diagram)*. Make 10 blocks.

Block Diagram

Quilt Assembly

1. Lay out blocks and navy print A squares as shown in *Quilt Top Assembly Diagram* on page 88. Join blocks into rows; join rows to complete quilt center.

2. Add 1 border to each side of quilt center. Add remaining borders to top and bottom of quilt.

Finishing

1. Divide backing into 2 (1⅝-yard) lengths. Join panels lengthwise. Seam will run horizontally.

2. Layer backing, batting, and quilt top; baste. Quilt as desired. Quilt shown was quilted with a snowflake design in the navy squares and overall meandering *(Quilting Diagram on page 88).*

3. Join 2½"-wide dark blue print strips into 1 continuous piece for straight-grain French-fold binding Add binding to quilt.

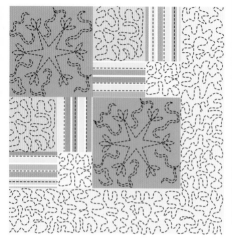

Quilting Diagram

SIZE OPTIONS

	Crib (40" × 40")	Twin (70" × 90")
Blocks	5	24
Setting	3 × 3	6 × 8

MATERIALS

Navy Print	¾ yard	2½ yards
Dark Blue Print	½ yard	¾ yard
Light Blue Print	1 yard	1½ yards
Medium Blue Print	¼ yard	⅞ yard
White Print	¼ yard	½ yard
Multi-Color Stripe	½ yard	1¼ yards
Backing Fabric	1¼ yards	5½ yards
Batting	Crib-size	Twin-size

 WEB EXTRA

Go to www.FonsandPorter.com/chillinsizes to download *Quilt Top Assembly Diagrams* for these size options.

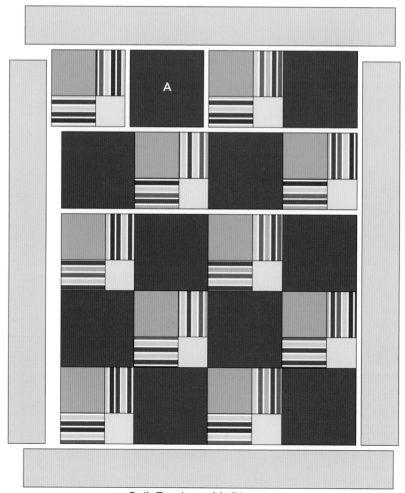

Quilt Top Assembly Diagram

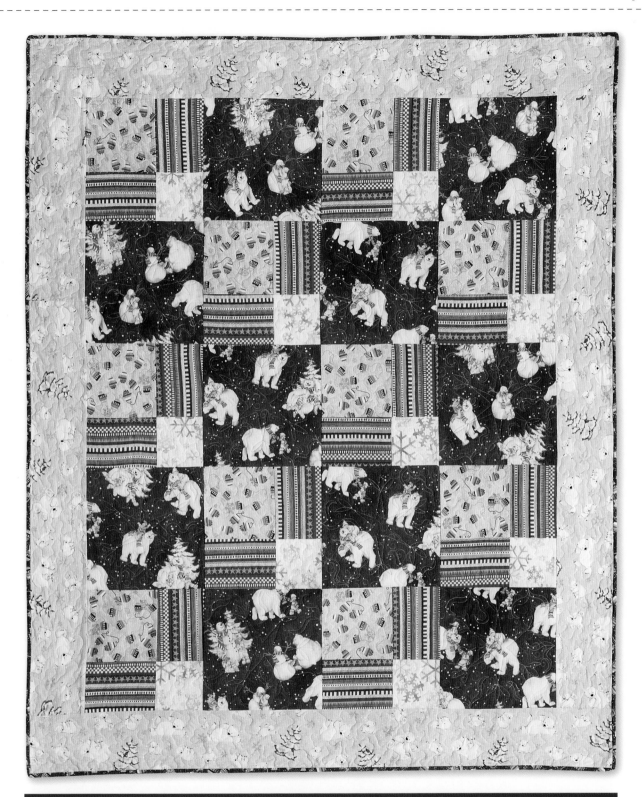

DESIGNER

Rochelle Martin has been a quilter for twenty years. She started her own pattern design business, Cottage Quilt Designs, in 2004. ✳

Early Frost

Make this quilt for your favorite wildlife enthusiast.
The realistic nature prints are by artist Jim Hansel.

PROJECT RATING: INTERMEDIATE

Size: 54½" × 79"

MATERIALS

1 Early Frost panel

1¾ yards Early Frost Stripe for top
and bottom borders

2¼ yards black print for sashing and
binding

2¼ yards dark brown print
for borders

⅜ yard green print

⅜ yard light gray print

⅜ yard dark gray print

⅜ yard medium brown print

4¾ yards backing fabric

Twin-size quilt batting

Cutting

Measurements include ¼" seam
allowances. Border strips are exact
length needed. You may want to make
them longer to allow for piecing
variations.

From Early Frost panel, cut:

• 1 (18½" × 23") rectangle,
  centering design.

• 2 (8½" × 6½") A rectangles.

• 2 (6½" × 8½") A rectangles.

From Early Frost stripe, cut:

• 2 (11"-wide) **lengthwise** strips. From
  strips, cut 2 (11" × 55") top and
  bottom outer borders.

> ### Sew **Smart**™
> Referring to photo on page 93, cut
> borders as shown. Top border will
> have narrow stripe on top; bottom
> border will have wide stripe on top.
> —Marianne

From black print, cut:

• 8 (2¼"-wide) strips for binding.

From remaining black print, cut:

• 11 (1¼"-wide) **lengthwise** strips.
  From strips, cut:

  • 2 (1¼" × 57") F rectangles.

  • 2 (1¼" × 55") G rectangles.

  • 4 (1¼" × 43½") D rectangles.

  • 2 (1¼" × 23") B rectangles.

  • 2 (1¼" × 20") C rectangles.

  • 16 (1¼" × 6½") E rectangles.

From dark brown print, cut:

• 2 (10"-wide) strips. From strips,
  cut 2 (10" × 30") top and bottom
  inner borders.

From remaining dark brown print, cut:

• 3 (5½"-wide) **lengthwise** strips. From
  strips, cut 2 (5½" × 57") side outer

borders and 2 (5½" × 24½") side
inner borders.

NOTE: The fabrics used in this quilt
are directional prints. For the center
rectangle and A rectangles, the first
number refers to the horizontal
measurement, and the second number
refers to the vertical measurement.

> ### Sew **Smart**™
> Referring to photo on page 93, cut
> designs as desired. Two Early Frost
> panel A rectangles will be horizontal
> and two will be vertical. —Marianne

From green print, cut:

• 3 (8½" × 6½") A rectangles.

• 2 (6½" × 8½") A rectangles.

From light gray print, cut:

• 2 (8½" × 6½") A rectangles.

• 2 (6½" × 8½") A rectangles.

From dark gray print, cut:

• 1 (8½" × 6½") A rectangle.

• 2 (6½" × 8½") A rectangles.

From medium brown print, cut:

• 2 (8½" × 6½") A rectangles.

• 2 (6½" × 8½") A rectangles.

Quilt Assembly

1. Referring to *Quilt Top Assembly Diagram*, add black print B rectangles to sides of center rectangle. Add black print C rectangles to top and bottom of center.

2. Repeat for dark brown inner borders.

3. Add 1 black print D rectangle to each side of quilt.

4. Lay out 5 (6½" × 8½") A rectangles and 4 black print E rectangles as shown in *Quilt Top Assembly Diagram*. (Refer to photo on page 93 for placement.) Join rectangles to make 1 pieced side border. Make 2 pieced side borders. Add borders to quilt.

5. Add black print D rectangles to top and bottom of quilt.

6. Lay out 5 (8½" × 6½") A rectangles and 4 black print E rectangles as shown in *Quilt Top Assembly Diagram*. (Refer to photo on page 93 for placement.) Join rectangles to make pieced top border. Repeat for pieced bottom border. Add borders to quilt.

7. Add black print F rectangles to sides of quilt. Add dark brown print outer borders to sides of quilt.

8. Add black print G rectangles to top and bottom of quilt.

9. Add stripe borders to top and bottom of quilt.

Finishing

1. Divide backing into 2 (2⅜-yard) lengths. Cut 1 piece in half lengthwise to make 2 narrow panels. Join 1 narrow panel to each side of wider panel; press seam allowances toward narrow panels.

2. Layer backing, batting, and quilt top; baste. Quilt as desired. Quilt shown was outline quilted around wildlife shapes in the rectangles, stitched in the ditch of borders, and has crosshatching in the brown borders *(Quilting Diagram)*.

3. Join 2¼"-wide black print print strips into 1 continuous piece for straight-grain French-fold binding. Add binding to quilt. ✳

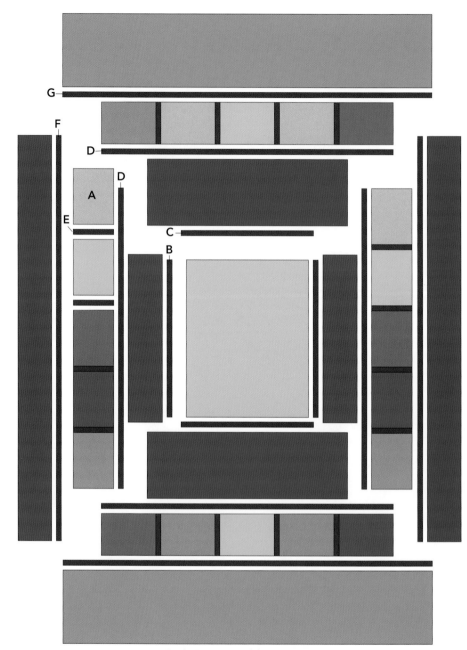

Quilt Top Assembly Diagram

Quilting Diagram

QUILT BY **Mari Sue Blacksmith**.
MACHINE QUILTED BY **Marietta Huggins**.

Cowboys

Cutting only squares and rectangles makes this quilt quick
and easy to assemble.

PROJECT RATING: EASY
Size: 53" × 69"
Blocks: 6 (12")
Square-in-a-Square blocks

MATERIALS

2½ yards cream print
1⅞ yards red print
1½ yards brown print
3½ yards backing fabric
Twin-size quilt batting

Cutting

Measurements include ¼" seam
allowances. Border strips are exact
length needed. You may want to make
them longer to allow for piecing
variations.

From cream print, cut:

• 2 (12½"-wide) strips. From strips, cut
6 (12½") A squares.

• 7 (3"-wide) strips. Piece strips to make
2 (3" × 64½") side border #4 and 2
(3" × 53½") top and bottom border #4.

• 12 (2½"-wide) strips. From strips, cut
68 (2½" × 6½") E rectangles.

From red print, cut:

• 7 (4½"-wide) strips. From strips, cut
12 (4½") C squares. Piece remaining
strips to make 2 (4½" × 54½") side
border #2 and 2 (4½" × 46½") top
and bottom border #2.

• 5 (2½"-wide) strips. From strips, cut
68 (2½") D squares.

• 7 (2¼"-wide) strips for binding.

From brown print, cut:

• 4 (6¼"-wide) strips. From strips, cut
24 (6¼") B squares.

• 11 (1½"-wide) strips. From strips, cut
2 (1½" × 38½") top and bottom border
#1. Piece remaining strips to make 2
(1½" × 62½") side border #3,
2 (1½" × 52½") side border #1,
and 2 (1½" × 48½") top and bottom
border #3.

Block Assembly

1. Referring to *Block Diagrams*, place 1
brown print B square atop 1 cream
print A square, right sides facing.
Stitch diagonally from corner to
corner as shown. Trim ¼" beyond
stitching. Press open to reveal triangle.
Repeat for remaining corners to complete 1 block.

2. Make 6 blocks.

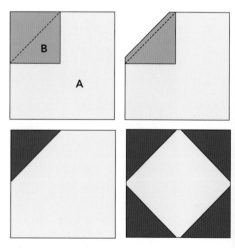

Block Diagrams

Sashing Assembly

1. Referring to *Sashing Unit Diagrams*, place 1 red print D square atop 1 cream print E rectangle, right sides facing. Stitch diagonally from corner to corner as shown. Trim ¼" beyond stitching. Press open to reveal triangle to complete 1 Sashing Unit. Make 34 Sashing Units.

Sashing Unit Diagrams

2. In the same manner, make 34 reversed Sashing Units, stitching D square to opposite corner *(Reversed Sashing Unit Diagrams)*.

Reversed Sashing Unit Diagrams

3. Join 2 Sashing Units and 2 reversed Sashing Units as shown in *Sashing Section Diagrams* to complete 1 Sashing Section. Make 17 Sashing Sections.

Sashing Section Diagrams

Quilt Assembly

1. Lay out blocks, sashing sections, and red print C squares as shown in *Quilt Top Assembly Diagram*. Join into rows; join rows to complete quilt center.

2. Add brown print border #1 to sides of quilt center. Add brown print top and bottom border #1 to quilt.

3. Repeat for red print border #2, brown print border #3, and cream print border #4.

Finishing

1. Divide backing into 2 (1¾-yard) lengths. Join panels lengthwise. Seam will run horizontally.

2. Layer backing, batting, and quilt top; baste. Quilt as desired. Quilt shown was quilted with an overall design *(Quilting Diagram)*.

3. Join 2¼"-wide red print strips into 1 continuous piece for straight-grain French-fold binding. Add binding to quilt.

Quilting Diagram

TRIED & TRUE

Highlight a retro print such as this one from the Apple collection by Timeless Treasures.

DESIGNER

Mari Sue Blacksmith always loved quilts, but never attempted to make one until a friend put her to the task. She has now made over 200 quilts. Mari Sue is an upper elementary teacher by day and a quilter by night. ✳

Quilt Top Assembly Diagram

Twin Size

Queen Size

SIZE OPTIONS

	Twin (69" × 85")	Queen (85" × 101")
Blocks	12	20
Sashing Sections	31	49

MATERIALS

Cream Print	3¾ yards	6 yards
Red Print	2¾ yards	3¾ yards
Brown Print	2¼ yards	3½ yards
Backing Fabric	5¼ yards	7¾ yards
Batting	Full-size	King-size

Space Ranger

Inspire a budding astronaut with this quilt made from space-theme fabrics.
Cutting triangles for the stars is easy with the Fons & Porter Half & Quarter Ruler.

PROJECT RATING: EASY

Size: 68" × 83"

Blocks: 12 (12") Star blocks

MATERIALS

2 yards dark blue print for blocks, outer border, and binding

1⅜ yards medium blue print for sashing

¾ yard light blue print for blocks

2½ yards navy print for blocks and middle border

1⅛ yards gray print for blocks and inner border

Fons & Porter Half & Quarter Ruler (optional)

5 yards backing fabric

Twin-size quilt batting

Cutting

Measurements include ¼" seam allowances. Border strips are exact length needed. You may want to make them longer to allow for piecing variations.

Sew Smart™

To cut A squares and half-square B triangles from the same size strips using the Fons & Porter Half & Quarter Ruler, see *Sew Easy: Cutting Half-Square Triangles* on page 105. If you are not using the Fons & Porter Half & Quarter Ruler follow cutting NOTES. —Liz

---

From dark blue print, cut:

• 2 (3½"-wide) strips. From strips, cut 14 (3½") A squares.

• 6 (3½"-wide) strips. From strips, cut 96 half-square B triangles.

   NOTE: If not using the Fons & Porter Half & Quarter Ruler to cut the B triangles, cut: 5 (3⅞"-wide) strips. From strips, cut 48 (3⅞") squares. Cut squares in half diagonally to make 96 half-square B triangles.

• 9 (2¼"-wide) strips for binding.

• 8 (1½"-wide) strips. Piece strips to make 2 (1½" × 81½") side outer borders and 2 (1½" × 68½") top and bottom outer borders.

From medium blue print, cut:

• 1 (5½"-wide) strip. From strip, cut 4 (5½") C squares.

• 11 (3½"-wide) strips. From strips, cut 31 (3½" × 12½") sashing rectangles.

From light blue print, cut:

• 3 (3½"-wide) strips. From strips, cut 30 (3½") A squares.

• 3 (3½"-wide) strips. From strips, cut 48 half-square B triangles.

   NOTE: If not using the Fons & Porter Half & Quarter Ruler to cut the B triangles, cut: 3 (3⅞"-wide) strips. From strips, cut 24 (3⅞") squares. Cut squares in half diagonally to make 48 half-square B triangles.

From navy print, cut:

• 7 (8½"-wide) strips. Piece strips to make 2 (8½" × 65½") side middle borders and 2 (8½" × 50½") top and bottom middle borders.

• 4 (3½"-wide) strips. From strips, cut 8 (3½" × 5½") D rectangles and 24 (3½") A squares.

- 3 (3½"-wide) strips. From strips, cut 48 half-square B triangles.

  NOTE: If not using the Fons & Porter Half & Quarter Ruler to cut the B triangles, cut: 3 (3⅞"-wide) strips. From strips, cut 24 (3⅞") squares. Cut squares in half diagonally to make 48 half-square B triangles.

From gray print, cut:

- 1 (3½"-wide) strip. From strip, cut 4 (3½") A squares.

- 6 (3½"-wide) strips. From strips, cut 96 half-square B triangles.

  NOTE: If not using the Fons & Porter Half & Quarter Ruler to cut the B triangles, cut: 5 (3⅞"-wide) strips. From strips, cut 48 (3⅞") squares. Cut squares in half diagonally to make 96 half-square B triangles.

- 7 (1½"-wide) strips. Piece strips to make 2 (1½" × 63½") side inner borders and 2 (1½" × 50½") top and bottom inner borders.

Block Assembly

1. Join 1 dark blue print B triangle and 1 navy print B triangle as shown in *Triangle-Square Diagrams*. Make 4 dark blue/navy triangle-squares.

Triangle-Square Diagrams

2. In the same manner, make 4 gray/navy triangle-squares using gray print and navy print B triangles, and 4 dark blue/gray triangle-squares using dark blue print and gray print B triangles.

3. Lay out triangle squares and 4 navy print A squares as shown in *Block Assembly Diagram*. Join into rows; join rows to complete 1 navy block (*Block Diagrams*). Make 6 navy blocks.

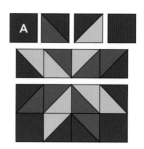

Block Assembly Diagram

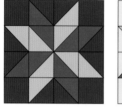 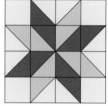

Block Diagrams

4. In the same manner, make 6 light blue blocks using light blue print A squares and light blue, medium blue, and gray print B triangles.

Quilt Assembly

1. Lay out blocks, dark blue and light blue print A squares, and medium blue print sashing rectangles as shown in *Quilt Top Assembly Diagram*. Join into rows; join rows to complete quilt center.

2. Add gray print side inner borders to quilt center. Add top and bottom inner borders to quilt.

3. Lay out 1 gray print A square, 1 medium blue print C square, and 2 navy print D rectangles as shown in *Corner Unit Diagrams* on page 103. Join into rows; join rows to complete 1 Corner Unit. Make 4 Corner Units.

4. Add navy print side middle borders to quilt. Add 1 Corner Unit to each end of top and bottom middle borders. Add borders to quilt.

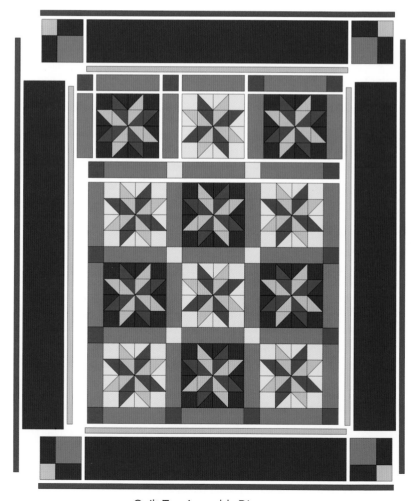

Quilt Top Assembly Diagram

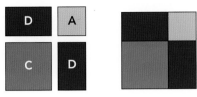

Corner Unit Diagrams

5. Add dark blue print side outer borders to quilt center. Add top and bottom outer borders to quilt.

Finishing

1. Divide backing into 2 (2½-yard) lengths. Cut 1 piece in half lengthwise to make 2 narrow panels. Join 1 narrow panel to each side of wider panel; press seam allowances toward narrow panels.

2. Layer backing, batting, and quilt top; baste. Quilt as desired. Quilt shown was quilted in the ditch, with loops in the middle border, and with stars in sashing squares (*Quilting Diagram*).

3. Join 2¼"-wide dark blue print strips into 1 continuous piece for straight-grain French-fold binding. Add binding to quilt.

Quilting Diagram

TRIED & TRUE

Sunny hot colors in Tonga Batiks from Timeless Treasures spice up this traditional block.

SIZE OPTIONS

	Throw (53" × 68")	Full (83" × 98")
Blocks	6	20
Setting	2 × 3	4 × 5

MATERIALS

	Throw (53" × 68")	Full (83" × 98")
Dark Blue Print	1½ yards	2¼ yards
Medium Blue Print	⅞ yard	2 yards
Light Blue Print	⅝ yard	1 yard
Navy Print	2 yards	3 yards
Gray Print	¾ yard	1½ yards
Backing Fabric	1½ yards	7½ yards
Batting	Twin-size	Queen-size

 WEB EXTRA

Go to www.FonsandPorter.com/spacesizes to download *Quilt Top Assembly Diagrams* for these size options.

DESIGNER

Designer Heidi Pridemore is known for her whimsical and fun quilts. In addition to creating quilts for several fabric companies, she teaches, designs fabric, and has authored three books. Heidi started her company in 1998, and has been joined by her husband and several other family members. ✳

Space Ranger Pillowcase

PROJECT RATING: EASY

Size: 19" × 30"

(Fits a standard bed pillow)

MATERIALS

¾ yard light blue print for
  pillowcase

¼ yard dark blue print for band

2"-wide strip accent fabric

Cutting

From light blue print, cut:

• 1 (27" × 40") rectangle.

From contrasting fabric, cut:

• 1 (9" × 40") strip.

From accent fabric, cut:

• 1 (2" × 40") strip.

Assembly

1. Referring to *Diagram 1*, fold
pillowcase fabric into a 20" × 27"
rectangle, with right sides facing. Stitch
along top and side edge with ½"
seam. Turn pillowcase right side out.

> ### Sew **Smart**™
> Zigzag, pink, or serge raw edges
> of seams to help prevent raveling
> during washing. —Marianne

2. With right sides facing, join short
ends of band strip with a ½" seam.
Press under ½" along 1 long edge
of band.

3. Join short ends of accent strip with
a ½" seam. Fold accent strip in half
with wrong sides facing; press.

4. Pin accent strip to right side of
pillowcase, aligning raw edges. Pin
contrasting band atop accent strip as
shown in *Diagram 2*. Stitch around
pillowcase through all layers with
a ½" seam. Press seam allowance
toward pillowcase.

5. Turn band to inside of pillowcase,
aligning fold of band with seam.
Press. Stitch in the ditch through all
layers *(Diagram 3)*.

Diagram 1

Diagram 2

Diagram 3

Cutting Half-Square Triangles

Easily cut half-square triangles for *Space Ranger* using the Fons & Porter Half & Quarter Ruler.

1. Straighten the left edge of fabric strip. Place the strip width line (3½" for *Space Rangers*) of the Fons & Porter Half & Quarter Ruler on the bottom edge of strip, aligning left edge of ruler with straightened edge of strip. The yellow tip of ruler will extend beyond top edge of strip.
2. Cut along right edge of ruler to make 1 half-square triangle (*Photo A*).
3. Turn ruler and align fabric-width line with top edge of strip. Cut along right edge of ruler (*Photo B*).
4. Repeat to cut required number of half-square triangles.

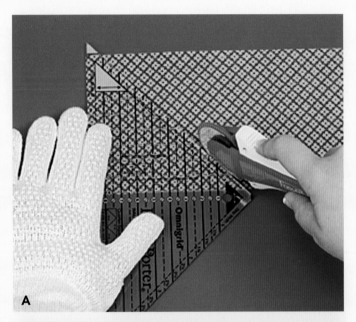

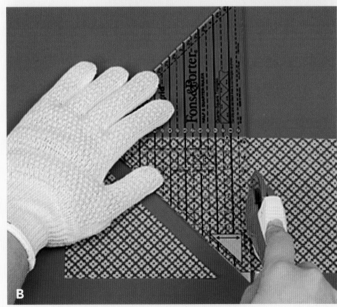

Speedy

With this quilt, heads or tails you win! Alabama quilter Kelly Davis cleverly combined fun, bright prints in this delightful quilt. The fabrics remind her of childhood summers and turtles bought at the dime store. The traditional Drunkard's Path pattern is a jumping-off place for Kelly's design—the three-dimensional heads and tails are stitched in the seams.

PROJECT RATING: CHALLENGING

Finished Size: 70" × 84"

Blocks: 20 (14") Turtle blocks

Note: The buttons on this quilt may present a choking hazard for small children.

MATERIALS

20 fat quarters★ assorted bright prints for turtles

2¾ yards white for block backgrounds

1½ yards green print for border

¾ yard blue print for binding

5 yards backing fabric

Freezer paper for templates or Fons & Porter's Curved Seam Template Set

40 (½"-diameter) black buttons for eyes

Twin-size batting

★fat quarter = 18" × 20"

Cutting

Use the large take-away and fill-in templates from Fons & Porter's Curved Seam Template Set, or make templates from freezer paper using the patterns on page 109. See *Sew Easy: Using Curved Seam Templates* on page 110 for instructions to rotary cut curved pieces. Pattern pieces for Head and Tail are on page 109. Measurements include ¼" seam allowances. Border strips are exact length needed. You may want to make them longer to allow for piecing variations.

From each bright print fat quarter, cut:

- 1 (2½"-wide) strip for pieced inner border.
- 2 (7½") squares for turtle leg sections. Use large take-away template to cut 1 A from each square.
- 2 (5½") squares for turtle head and tail sections. Use large fill-in template to cut 1 B quarter-circle from each square.
- 2 Heads.
- 2 Tails.

From white background fabric, cut:

- 8 (7½"-wide) strips. From strips, cut 40 (7½") squares. Use large take-away template to cut 1 A from each square.

- 6 (5½"-wide) strips. From strips, cut 40 (5½") squares. Use large fill-in template to cut 1 B quarter-circle from each square.

From green print border fabric, cut:

- 8 (5½"-wide) strips. Piece strips to make 2 (5½" × 74½") side borders and 2 (5½" × 70½") top and bottom borders.

From blue print fabric, cut:

- 9 (2¼"-wide) strips for binding.

Block Assembly

1. Place 2 matching head pieces right sides facing. Stitch using ¼" seam; leave bottom edge open for turning. Turn head right side out. Sew buttons for eyes on right side of head at each X. (For small children, embroider eyes or color with permanent marker.) Make 20 heads.

2. Place 2 matching tail pieces right sides facing. Stitch using ¼" seam; leave bottom edge open for turning. Turn tail right side out. Make 20 tails.

3. Referring to *Piecing Diagrams*, place 1 head atop 1 matching B, right sides together, matching dot on head to center of curve. Place 1 white A atop head, right side down, matching center of curve to dot on head piece. Refer to *Sew Easy: Sewing Curved Seams* on page 111 to pin and sew pieces together to complete 1 head section. Make 1 head section from each turtle fabric.

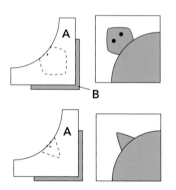

Piecing Diagrams

4. In the same manner, join 1 tail piece, 1 white A, and 1 bright B together to make 1 tail section. Make 1 tail section from each turtle fabric.

5. Referring to *Block Diagram*, join 1 bright print A to 1 background B to make 1 leg section. Make 2 leg sections from each turtle fabric.

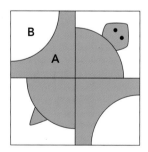

Block Diagram

6. Referring to *Block Diagram*, lay out 1 head section, 1 tail section, and 2 leg sections in matching fabric. Join into rows; join rows to complete 1 Turtle block. Make 20 Turtle blocks.

Quilt Assembly

1. Lay out blocks as shown in photo. Join into rows; join rows to complete quilt center.

2. Cut (2½"-wide) bright print strips into random lengths ranging from 8"–18" long. Piece rectangles to make 2 (2½" × 70½") side inner borders and 2 (2½" × 60½") top and bottom inner borders. Add side inner borders to quilt center. Add top and bottom inner borders to quilt.

3. Add green print side outer borders to quilt center. Add green print top and bottom outer borders to quilt.

Finishing

1. Divide backing into 2 (2½-yard) lengths. Cut 1 piece in half lengthwise. Sew 1 narrow panel to each side of wide panel. Press seam allowances toward narrow panels.

2. Layer backing, batting, and quilt top; baste. Quilt as desired. The quilt shown was quilted with a spiral on each turtle shell, wavy water-like stippling in the background, swirls on the inner border, and dragonflies in the outer border.

3. Join 2¼"-wide blue print strips into 1 continuous piece for straight-grain French-fold binding. Add binding to quilt.

DESIGNER

Designer Kelly Davis learned to quilt before she could read. Her teacher, grandmother Elnora Kelly, helped Kelly draw and cut patterns from paper grocery bags and choose fabric from her trash cans full of scraps. ❋

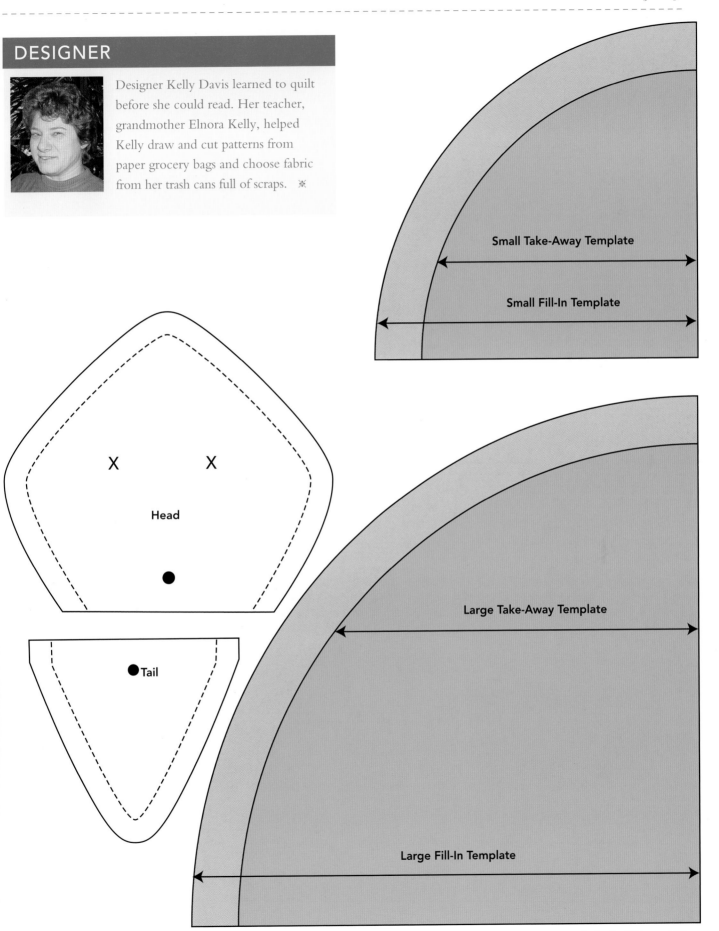

Small Take-Away Template

Small Fill-In Template

X   X

Head

●

●Tail

Large Take-Away Template

Large Fill-In Template

Sew *Easy*™

Using Curved Seam Templates

Fons & Porter's Curved Seam Template Set makes rotary cutting curved pieces easy. The red templates in the set are take-away templates, and the gray ones are fill-in templates. If you prefer to make your own templates, trace the take-away and fill-in patterns on page 109 onto freezer paper, and cut out shapes.

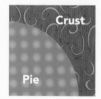

Sew **Smart**™

If you are using a freezer paper template, press it to the fabric square and cut with scissors. —Liz

Cutting the Basic Drunkard's Path Unit

1. From each of 2 contrasting fabrics, cut a square ½" larger than the desired finished block. For example, for a 6" block, cut 6½" squares.

2. Position the large red take-away template in 1 corner of the square that will be the background. Cut along the curved edge of the template (*Photo A*). The background is the piece remaining from the original square. The quarter circle may be discarded or saved to use as a scrap.

3. Position large gray fill-in template on remaining square and cut along curved edge (*Photo B*). Use the quarter circle to fill in the opening in the background. Remaining piece may be discarded or saved to use as a scrap.

4. To join pieces, see *Sew Easy: Sewing Curved Seams* on page 111.

Making a Basic Donut Unit

1. Begin by making a basic Drunkard's Path unit.

2. Place small red take-away template in corner of quarter-circle. Cut along the curved edge of template (*Photo C*). Discard quarter circle.

3. Use small gray fill-in template to cut a small quarter circle from scraps (*Photo D*).

4. To join pieces, see *Sew Easy: Sewing Curved Seams* on page 111.

Sewing Curved Seams

When you're making a Drunkard's Path or any quilt with curved pieces, use these tips to make sewing curved seams easier.

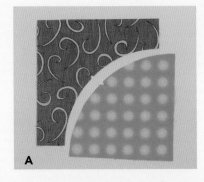

1. After cutting the background and the quarter-circle pieces, mark the center of the curve on each piece by folding in half and creasing or making a small clip (Photo A).

2. Working with the background on top, pin pieces together at curve centers, taking a small bite. At the end of the seam, align pieces and pin, taking a large bite (Photo B).

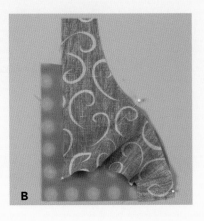

3. Align pieces at beginning of seam. Stitch to the middle of the curve. Use your fingertips to keep curved edges aligned or control the top fabric and keep edges aligned with a wooden skewer (Photo C).

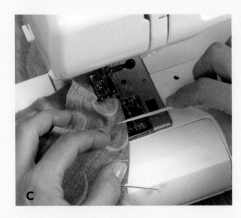

4. Leaving the needle in the fabric, raise the presser foot. "Fluff" the top fabric back toward where you have sewn (Photo D).

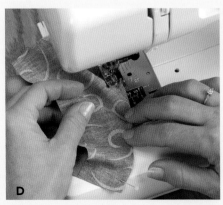

5. Align curved edges for the second half of the seam and stitch to about 1" from end of seam. Stop again and "fluff" the top fabric so ending edges are also aligned. Sew to the end of the seam (Photo E).

6. Gently press seam allowance toward background.

QUILT BY **Linda Hogan**.

Penguin Party

Liven up baby's nursery with this quilt of jaunty penguins in brightly colored vests.

PROJECT RATING: INTERMEDIATE
Size: 45½" × 45½"
Blocks: 9 (8½") Penguin blocks

MATERIALS

9 (5") squares assorted prints
  for Vests
13 (3") squares assorted prints
  for Balloons
¼ yard white solid for Bodies
  and Heads
1 fat quarter★ black pin dot
  for Fins
1 (4") square orange solid for Noses
1½ yards light blue solid for
  background
⅝ yard dark blue solid for sashing
1 yard black print for border
⅜ yard yellow solid for binding
2¾ yards backing fabric
Paper-backed fusible web
Assorted colors embroidery floss
Twin-size quilt batting
★fat quarter = 18" × 20"

Cutting

Measurements include ¼" seam allowances. Border strips are exact length needed. You may want to make them longer to allow for piecing variations. Patterns for appliqué are on page 117. Follow manufacturer's instructions for using fusible web.

From each (5") square, cut:
• 1 Vest.

From each (3") square, cut:
• 1 Balloon.

NOTE: If border fabric is a balloon print, cut 13 balloons from that fabric after cutting borders.

From white solid, cut:
• 9 Bodies.
• 9 Heads.

From black pin dot, cut:
• 9 Short Fins.
• 9 Short Fins Reversed.
• 9 Long Fins.

From (4") orange solid square, cut:
• 9 Noses.

From light blue solid, cut:
• 3 (9"-wide) strips. From strips, cut 9 (9") squares.

Bill Martin Jr / Eric Carle

• 7 (2½"-wide) strips. From 3 strips, cut 12 (2½" × 9") C rectangles. Remaining strips are for strip sets.

From dark blue solid, cut:

• 16 (1"-wide) strips. From 8 strips, cut 8 (1" × 38") sashing strips. Remaining strips are for strip sets.

From black print, cut:

• 5 (4½"-wide) strips. From strips, cut 2 (4½" × 38") side borders. Piece remaining strips to make 2 (4½" × 46") top and bottom borders.

From yellow solid, cut:

• 5 (2¼"-wide) strips for binding.

Block Assembly

1. Position pieces for 1 Penguin atop 1 (9") light blue square as shown in *Block Diagram*. Fuse in place.

Block Diagram

2. Machine appliqué pieces using matching thread to complete 1 Penguin block. Make 9 blocks.
3. Satin stitch eyes on penguins *(Satin Stitch Diagram)*.

Satin Stitch Diagram

Sashing Assembly

1. Join 1 (2½"-wide) light blue strip and 2 (1"-wide) dark blue strips as shown in *Strip Set Diagrams*. Make 4 Strip Sets.

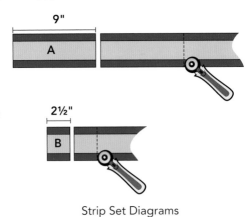

Strip Set Diagrams

2. From strip sets, cut 12 (9"-wide) A segments and 16 (2½"-wide) B segments.

Quilt Assembly

1. Lay out Penguin blocks, A and B segments, light blue C rectangles, and dark blue sashing strips as shown in *Quilt Top Assembly Diagram*.
2. Join into rows; join rows to complete quilt center.
3. Add black print side borders to quilt center. Add top and bottom borders to quilt.
4. Referring to quilt photo on page 116, position balloons on quilt top. Fuse in place. Machine appliqué

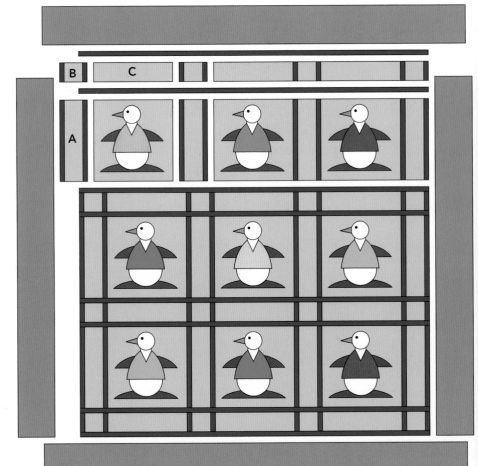

Quilt Top Assembly Diagram

balloons using matching thread. Stem stitch balloon strings using 3 strands of embroidery floss *(Stem Stitch Diagram)*.

Stem Stitch Diagram

Finishing

1. Divide backing into 2 (1⅜-yard) lengths. Cut 1 piece in half lengthwise to make 2 narrow panels. Join 1 narrow panel to wider panel. Remaining panel is extra and can be used to make a hanging sleeve.

2. Layer backing, batting, and quilt top; baste. Quilt as desired. Quilt shown was quilted in the ditch and with an orange peel design in the border *(Quilting Diagram)*.

3. Join 2¼"-wide yellow strips into 1 continuous piece for straight-grain French-fold binding. Add binding to quilt.

Quilting Diagram

TRIED & TRUE

Prints from the Serendipity Sunflowers collection by RJR Fabrics dress up this little penguin perfectly.

DESIGNER

Longarm quilter Linda Hogan has been teaching beginning quilting classes for many years. She especially enjoys machine appliqué, and, when she found balloon fabric, she knew it would be perfect for her appliquéd *Penguin Party* quilt. ✳

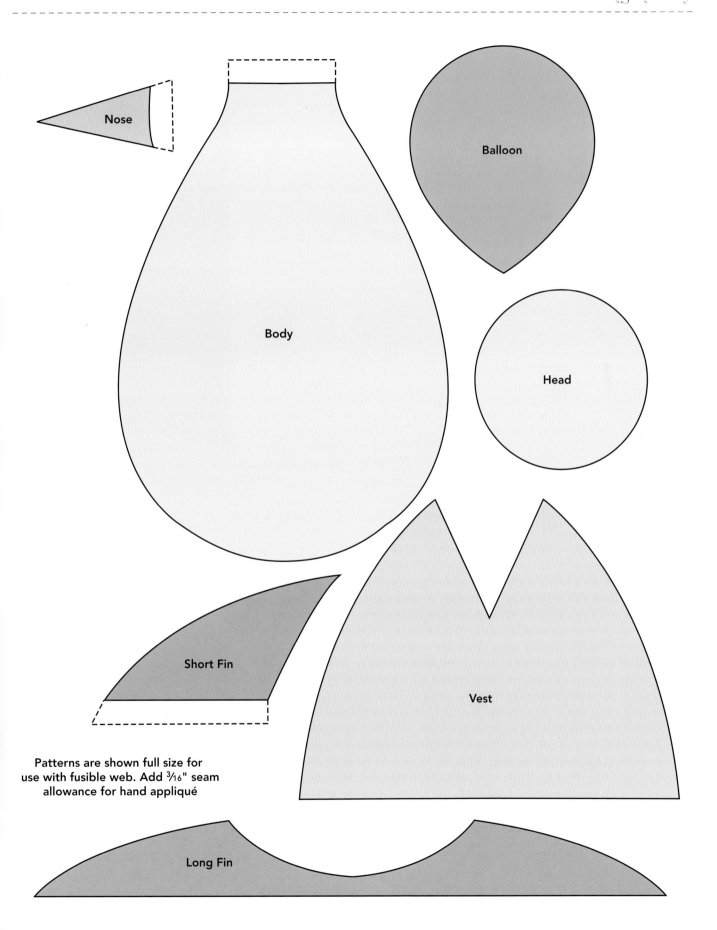

Nose

Body

Balloon

Head

Short Fin

Vest

Patterns are shown full size for use with fusible web. Add ³⁄₁₆" seam allowance for hand appliqué

Long Fin

Ziggity Zaggity

Designer Sharon Smith made this fun quilt using a collection of pre-cut 2½"-wide strips.

PROJECT RATING: INTERMEDIATE
Size: 47¾" × 47"

MATERIALS

30 (2½" × 40") strips assorted prints
⅝ yard red solid for inner border and binding
1½ yards multicolor stripe for outer border
3 yards backing fabric
Twin-size quilt batting

Cutting

Refer to *Sew Easy: Cutting Parallelograms* on page 123 for instructions to cut parallelograms, or make a parallelogram template from the pattern on page 121. Measurements include ¼" seam allowances. Border strips are exact length needed. You may want to make them longer to allow for piecing variations.

From each assorted print strip, cut:
• 4 Parallelograms.
• 4 Parallelograms reversed.

> ### Sew **Smart**™
> Fold 2½"-wide strip in half with right sides facing. Cut through both layers to cut 1 parallelogram and 1 parallelogram reversed at the same time. —Liz

From red solid, cut:
• 5 (1½"-wide) strips. Piece strips to make 2 (1½" × 40½") side inner borders and 2 (1½" × 43¼") top and bottom inner borders.
• 5 (2¼"-wide) strips for binding.

From multicolor stripe, cut:
• 3 (3"-wide) strips. Piece strips to make 2 (3" × 48¼") top and bottom outer borders.
• 2 (3"-wide) **lengthwise** strips. From strips, cut 2 (3" × 42½") side outer borders.

Quilt Assembly

1. Referring to *Quilt Top Assembly Diagram*, join 12 assorted parallelograms to make 1 Row 1. Make 2 matching Row 1.

2. In the same manner, join 12 assorted reverse parallelograms to make Row 2. Make 2 matching Row 2.

3. Repeat Steps #1 and #2 to make 5 sets of 2 matching Row 1 and 2 matching Row 2.

4. Join rows, alternating Row 1 and Row 2, to complete quilt center. Straighten sides of quilt by trimming ¼" outside the pieced parallelograms.

5. Add red side inner borders to quilt center. Add red top and bottom inner borders to quilt.

6. Repeat for stripe outer borders.

Finishing

1. Divide backing into 2 (1½-yard) lengths. Cut 1 piece in half lengthwise to make 2 narrow panels. Join 1 narrow panel to wider panel. Remaining panel is extra and can be used to make a hanging sleeve.

2. Layer backing, batting, and quilt top; baste. Quilt as desired. Quilt shown was quilted with a vertical wave in the quilt center, in the ditch in the inner border, and with squiggles in the outer border *(Quilting Diagram on page 121)*.

3. Join 2¼"-wide red solid strips into 1 continuous piece for straight-grain French-fold binding. Add binding to quilt.

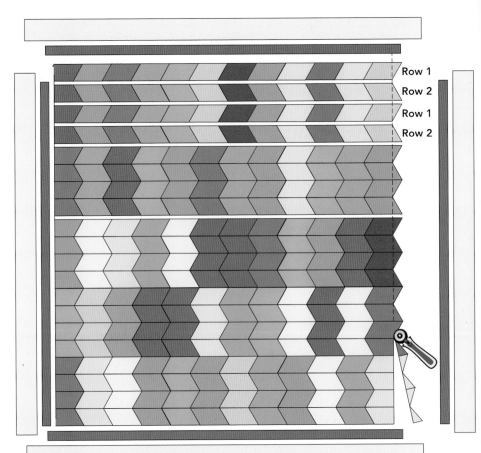

Quilt Top Assembly Diagram

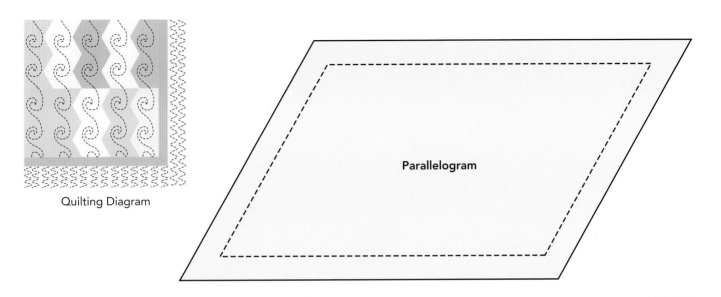

Quilting Diagram

Parallelogram

TRIED & TRUE

We stitched our version with prints from
the Royal Holiday collection by Deb Strain for Moda.

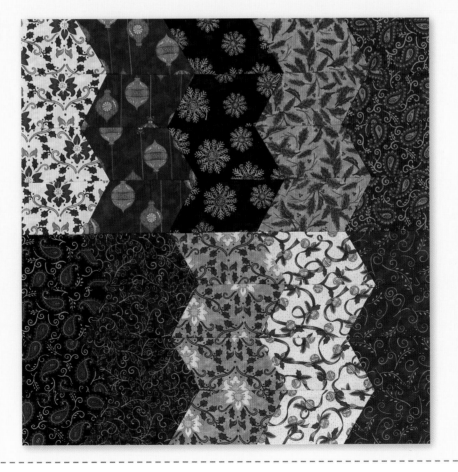

DESIGNER

Quilt designer Sharon Smith designs quilts, punchneedle projects, and penny rugs. She enjoyed making this simple quilt from a Jelly Roll and said it was a pleasure to watch it evolve. ✳

Cutting Parallelograms

Use this easy method to quickly cut parallelograms for *Ziggity Zaggity*.

1. Cut strip width for your project. (For *Ziggity Zaggity*, cut strips 2½" wide.)
2. Using ruler, trim end of strip at 60° angle (*Photo A*).
3. Position desired line of ruler on angled edge. (For *Ziggity Zaggity*, use 3½" line.) Cut along edge of ruler to make 1 parallelogram (*Photo B*).
4. Continue in this manner to cut desired number of parallelograms.

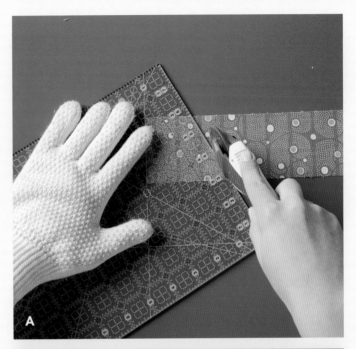

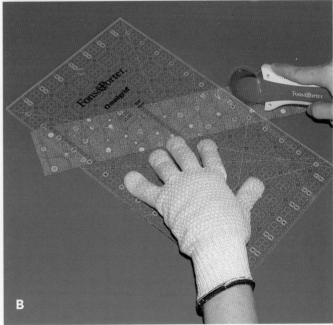

Diamonds in the Blue

Bring back childhood memories as you make this quilt with blue skies, bright kites, and billowy clouds!

PROJECT RATING: INTERMEDIATE
Size: 40" × 47"
Blocks: 10 (8" × 11") Kite blocks

MATERIALS

10 fat eighths★ assorted prints in red, yellow, green, and blue
10 fat eighths★ assorted solids in yellow, green, blue, orange, and pink
2¼ yards blue print for background
Template material
Paper-backed fusible web
½ yard white print for binding
2¾ yards backing fabric
Crib-size quilt batting
★fat eighth = 9" × 20"

Cutting

Measurements include ¼" seam allowances. Border strips are exact length needed. You may want to make them longer to allow for piecing variations. Patterns are on pages 126–129. Follow manufacturer's instructions for using fusible web.

From assorted prints and solids, cut a total of:

- 4 A and 4 matching B.
- 4 C and 4 matching D.
- 4 A reversed and 4 matching B reversed.
- 4 C reversed and 4 matching D reversed.
- 2 J and 2 J reversed.
- 4 (4⅞") squares, matching J triangles. Cut squares in half diagonally to make 4 half-square I triangles (one of each is extra).

From remainders of prints and solids, cut:

- 10 (¾" × 9") strips for kite tails.
- 10 sets of 3 matching Bows.

From blue print, cut:

- 5 (8½"-wide) strips. From strips, cut 2 (8½" × 14½") N rectangles, 5 (8½" × 11½") L rectangles, 3 (8½" × 9½") M rectangles, and 3 (8½" × 5½") K rectangles.
- 4 E and 4 E reversed.
- 4 F and 4 F reversed.
- 4 G and 4 G reversed.
- 4 H and 4 H reversed.
- 2 J and 2 J reversed.
- 1 (4⅞"-wide) strip. From strip, cut 2 (4⅞") squares. Cut squares in half diagonally to make 4 half-square I triangles.

From white print, cut:

- 5 (2¼"-wide) strips for binding.

Block Assembly

1. Choose 1 set of matching A and B, matching C and D, and 1 each blue print E, F, G, and H. Join pieces to make units as shown in *Unit Diagrams*.

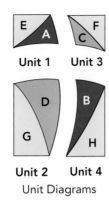

Unit 1 Unit 3

Unit 2 Unit 4

Unit Diagrams

2. Lay out units as shown in *Kite Block #1 Assembly Diagram*. Make 4 Kite Block #1 (*Kite Block #1 Diagram*).

Kite Block #1 Assembly Diagram

Kite Block #1 Diagram

3. In the same manner, make 4 Kite block #2 (*Kite Block #2 Diagram*).

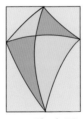

Kite Block #2 Diagram

4. Choose 1 set of 1 print I triangle and 1 matching print J triangle, and 1 solid I triangle and 1 matching solid J triangle, 2 blue print I triangles, and 2 blue print J triangles. Join print I triangle and 1 blue print I triangle as shown in *Triangle-Square Diagrams*. Repeat with solid I triangle and 1 blue print I triangle.

Triangle-Square Diagrams

5. Join 1 print J triangle and 1 blue print J triangle as shown in *Pieced Rectangle Diagrams*. Repeat with solid J triangle and 1 blue print J triangle.

Pieced Rectangle Diagrams

6. Lay out triangle-squares and pieced rectangles as shown in *Kite Block #3 Assembly Diagram*. Join into rows; join rows to complete 1 Kite Block #3 (*Kite Block #3 Diagram*). Make 2 Kite Block #3.

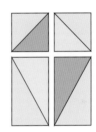 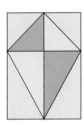

Kite Block #3 Assembly Diagram

Kite Block #3 Diagram

Quilt Assembly

1. Lay out Kite blocks and blue print K, L, M, and N rectangles as shown in *Quilt Top Assembly Diagram* on page 126.

2. Join into vertical rows; join rows.

3. Press each kite tail strip into thirds lengthwise, right side out. Referring to quilt photo on page 124, position kite tails on quilt top; machine appliqué in place using contrasting thread and small zigzag stitch.

4. Position 3 matching bows on each kite tail and appliqué in place.

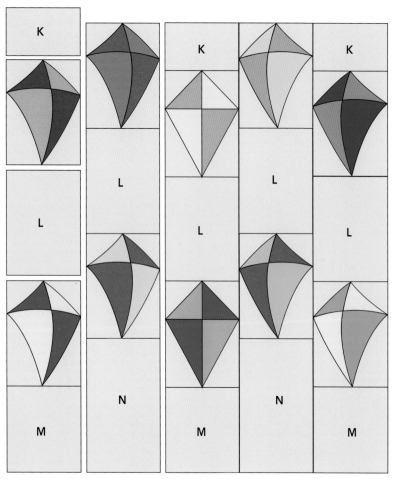

Quilt Top Assembly Diagram

DESIGNER

Sandy Smith and her husband enjoy spending time together flying kites. When their fellow kite-flying friends announced they were expecting a baby, Sandy designed this quilt for them. She drew kites that look as if they are about to be carried away by the wind. ✳

Finishing

1. Divide backing into 2 (1⅜-yard) lengths. Cut 1 piece in half lengthwise to make 2 narrow panels. Join 1 narrow panel to wider panel. Remaining panel is extra and can be used to make a hanging sleeve.

2. Layer backing, batting, and quilt top; baste. Quilt as desired. Quilt shown was quilted in the ditch around kites, tails, and bows, and with cloud shapes in the background *(Quilting Diagram)*.

3. Join 2¼"-wide white print strips into 1 continuous piece for straight-grain French-fold binding. Add binding to quilt.

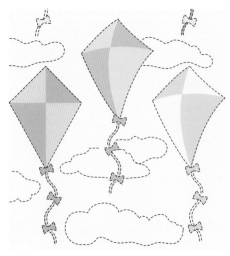

Quilting Diagram

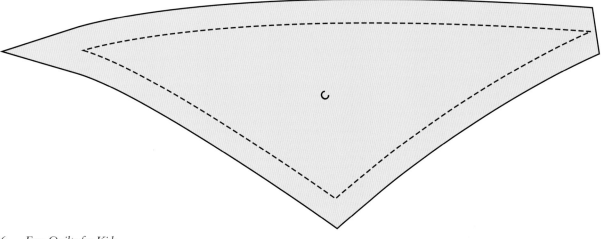

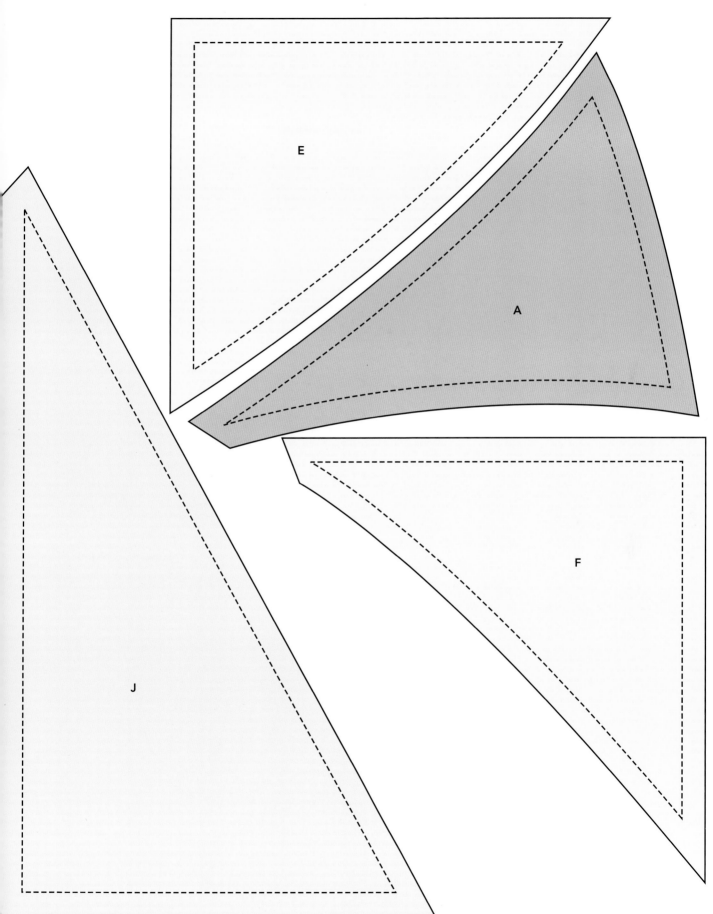

E

A

F

J

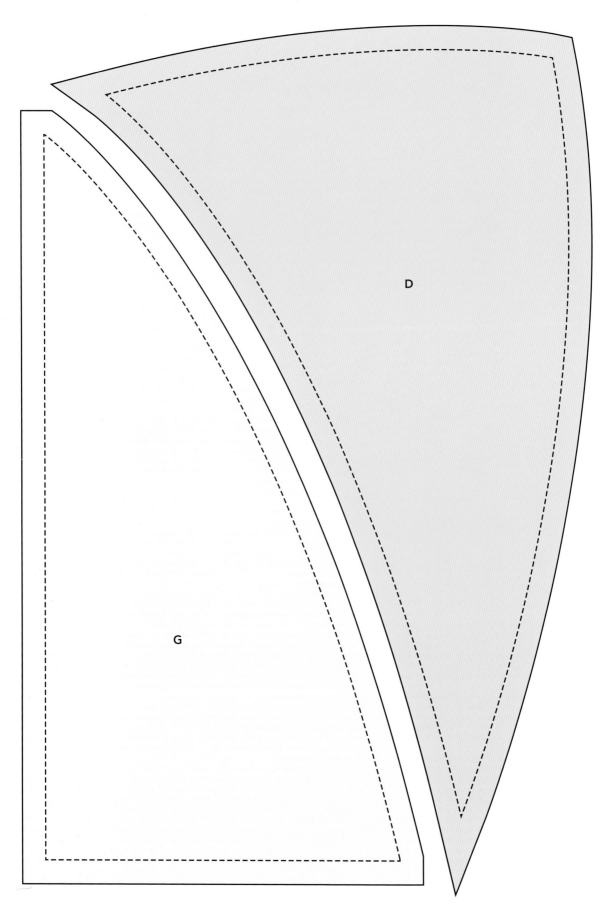

D

G

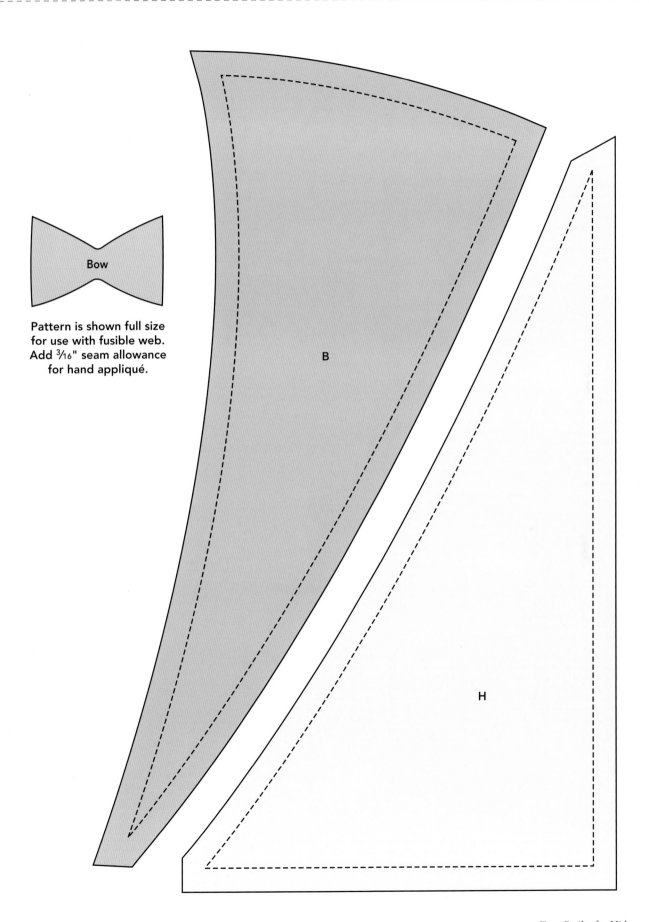

Bow

Pattern is shown full size
for use with fusible web.
Add ³⁄₁₆" seam allowance
for hand appliqué.

B

H

Magic Castle

Charming play panels easily turn a standard card table into a
magical castle for the little princess in your life.

PROJECT RATING: EASY
Size: fits a standard card table
(34" square × 28" high)

MATERIALS

1 magic castle panel
2 yards castle stripe
2¾ yards green print #1
2 yards green print #2

Cutting

NOTE: If your card table is a different
size, adjust cutting measurements
accordingly.

Measurements include ¼" seam
allowances.

From magic castle panel, cut:
• 2 (17½"-wide × 28½"-tall) A rectangles.

From castle stripe, cut:
• 3 (13½" × 35") **lengthwise** B rectangles.

From green print #1, cut:
• 1 (35" × 49½") C rectangle.
• 2 (17½" × 28½") A rectangles.
• 3 (1¾" -wide) strips. From strips, cut
  3 (1¾" × 35") hem facings.

From green print #2, cut:
• 1 (35" × 64½") D rectangle.

Tent Assembly

1. Place 1 green print A rectangle and 1 castle panel A rectangle right sides together. Join on sides and bottom, leaving top edge open. Clip corners, turn right side out, and press. Repeat for remaining castle panel.

2. Press under ¼" along 1 long edge of 1 hem facing strip. Align long raw edge of hem facing strip with bottom edge of 1 castle stripe B rectangle; stitch with ¼" seam. Turn up hem facing at seam. Topstitch close to pressed edge. Repeat with remaining castle stripe rectangles and hem facing strips.

3. Referring to *Tent Front/Back Assembly Diagram*, join castle panels to one end of green print C rectangle as shown. Add 1 hemmed castle stripe piece to opposite end.

Sew **Smart**™

Zigzag or serge close to edges of seam allowances to clean finish raw edges. —Marianne

4. Press under ¼", then ¼" again along long edges of tent front/back. Top-stitch close to first fold.

5. In the same manner, join 1 hemmed castle stripe piece to each end of green print D rectangle *(Tent Sides Assembly Diagram)*. Hem long edges.

6. Center tent sides atop card table. Place tent front/back atop tent sides.

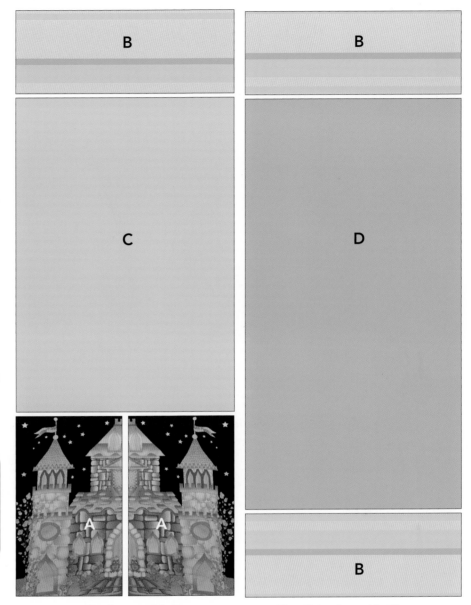

Tent Front/Back Assembly Diagram

Tent Sides Assembly Diagram

General Instructions

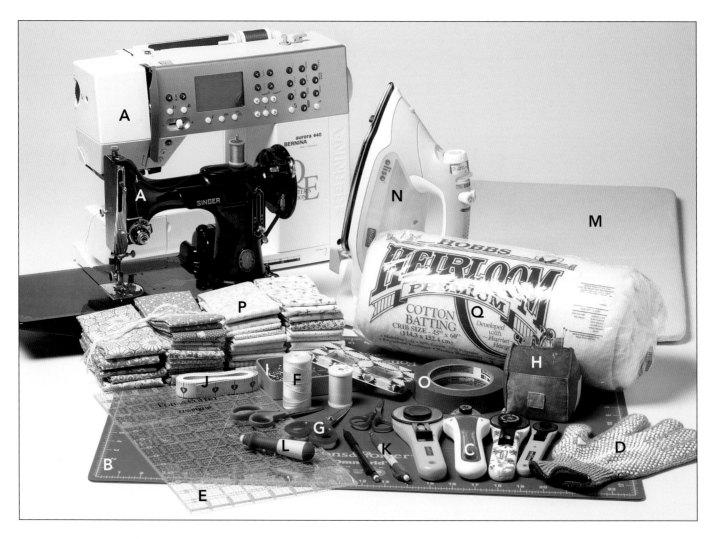

Basic Supplies

You'll need a **sewing machine (A)** in good working order to construct patchwork blocks, join blocks together, add borders, and machine quilt. We encourage you to purchase a machine from a local dealer, who can help you with service in the future, rather than from a discount store. Another option may be to borrow a machine from a friend or family member. If the machine has not been used in a while, have it serviced by a local dealer to make sure it is in good working order. If you need an extension cord, one with a surge protector is a good idea.

A **rotary cutting mat (B)** is essential for accurate and safe rotary cutting. Purchase one that is no smaller than 18" × 24".

Rotary cutting mats are made of "self-healing" material that can be used over and over.

A **rotary cutter (C)** is a cutting tool that looks like a pizza cutter, and has a very sharp blade. We recommend starting with a standard size 45mm rotary cutter. Always lock or close your cutter when it is not in use, and keep it out of the reach of children.

A **safety glove** (also known as a *Klutz Glove*) **(D)** is also recommended. Wear your safety glove on the hand that is holding the ruler in place. Because it is made of cut-resistant material, the safety glove protects your non-cutting hand from accidents that can occur if your cutting hand slips while cutting.

An acrylic **ruler (E)** is used in combination with your cutting mat and rotary cutter. We recommend the Fons & Porter

8" × 14" ruler, but a 6" × 12" ruler is another good option. You'll need a ruler with inch, quarter-inch, and eighth-inch markings that show clearly for ease of measuring. Choose a ruler with 45-degree-angle, 30-degree-angle, and 60-degree-angle lines marked on it as well.

Since you will be using 100% cotton fabric for your quilts, use **cotton or cotton-covered polyester thread (F)** for piecing and quilting. Avoid 100% polyester thread, as it tends to snarl.

Keep a pair of small **scissors (G)** near your sewing machine for cutting threads.

Thin, good quality **straight pins (H)** are preferred by quilters. The pins included with pin cushions are normally too thick to use for piecing, so discard them. Purchase a box of nickel-plated brass **safety pins** size #1 **(I)** to use for pin-basting the layers of your quilt together for machine quilting.

Invest in a 120"-long dressmaker's **measuring tape (J)**. This will come in handy when making borders for your quilt.

A 0.7–0.9mm mechanical **pencil (K)** works well for marking on your fabric.

Invest in a quality sharp **seam ripper (L)**. Every quilter gets well-acquainted with her seam ripper!

Set up an **ironing board (M)** and **iron (N)** in your sewing area. Pressing yardage before cutting, and pressing patchwork seams as you go are both essential for quality quiltmaking. Select an iron that has steam capability.

Masking **tape (O)** or painter's tape works well to mark your sewing machine so you can sew an accurate ¼" seam. You will also use tape to hold your backing fabric taut as you prepare your quilt sandwich for machine quilting.

The most exciting item that you will need for quilting is **fabric (P)**. Quilters generally prefer 100% cotton fabrics for their quilts. This fabric is woven from cotton threads, and has a lengthwise and a crosswise grain. The term "bias" is used to describe the diagonal grain of the fabric. If you make a 45-degree angle cut through a square of cotton fabric, the cut edges will be bias edges, which are quite stretchy. As you learn more quiltmaking techniques, you'll learn how bias can work to your advantage or disadvantage.

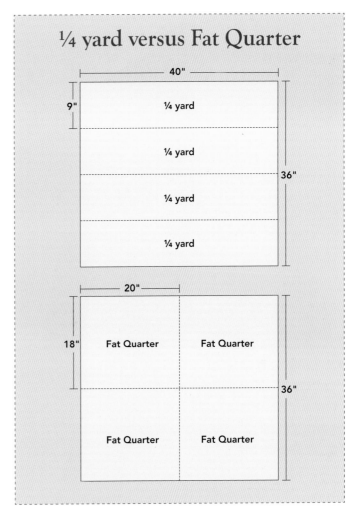

¼ yard versus Fat Quarter

Fabric is sold by the yard at quilt shops and fabric stores. Quilting fabric is generally about 40"–44" wide, so a yard is about 40" wide by 36" long. As you collect fabrics to build your own personal stash, you will buy yards, half yards (about 18" × 40"), quarter yards (about 9" × 40"), as well as other lengths.

Many quilt shops sell "fat quarters," a special cut favored by quilters. A fat quarter is created by cutting a half yard down the fold line into two 18" × 20" pieces (fat quarters) that are sold separately. Quilters like the nearly square shape of the fat quarter because it is more useful than the narrow regular quarter yard cut.

Batting (Q) is the filler between quilt top and backing that makes your quilt a quilt. It can be cotton, polyester, cotton-polyester blend, wool, silk, or other natural materials, such as bamboo or corn. Make sure the batting you buy is at least six inches wider and six inches longer than your quilt top.

Accurate Cutting

Measuring and cutting accuracy are important for successful quilting. Measure at least twice, and cut once!

Cut strips across the fabric width unless directed otherwise.

Cutting for patchwork usually begins with cutting strips, which are then cut into smaller pieces. First, cut straight strips from a fat quarter:

1. Fold fat quarter in half with selvage edge at the top (*Photo A*).

2. Straighten edge of fabric by placing ruler atop fabric, aligning one of the lines on ruler with selvage edge of fabric (*Photo B*). Cut along right edge of ruler.

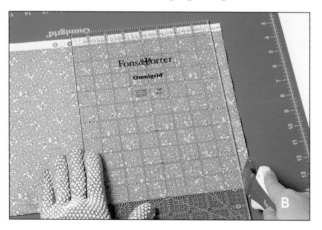

3. Rotate fabric, and use ruler to measure from cut edge to desired strip width (*Photo C*). Measurements in instructions include ¼" seam allowances.
4. After cutting the required number of strips, cut strips into squares and label them.

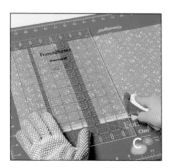

Setting up Your Sewing Machine

Sew Accurate ¼" Seams

Standard seam width for patchwork and quiltmaking is ¼". Some machines come with a patchwork presser foot, also known as a quarter-inch foot. If your machine doesn't have a quarter-inch foot, you may be able to purchase one from a dealer. Or, you can create a quarter-inch seam guide on your machine using masking tape or painter's tape.

Place an acrylic ruler on your sewing machine bed under the presser foot. Slowly turn handwheel until the tip of the needle barely rests atop the ruler's quarter-inch mark (*Photo A*). Make sure the lines on the ruler are parallel to the lines on the machine throat plate. Place tape on the machine bed along edge of ruler (*Photo B*).

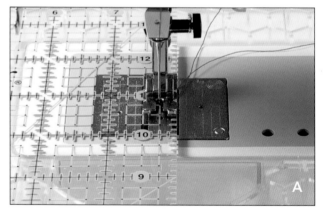

Take a Simple Seam Test

Seam accuracy is critical to machine piecing, so take this simple test once you have your quarter-inch presser foot on your machine or have created a tape guide.

Place 2 (2½") squares right sides together, and sew with a scant ¼" seam. Open squares and finger press seam. To finger press, with right sides facing you, press the seam to one side with your fingernail. Measure across pieces, raw edge to raw edge (*Photo C*). If they measure 4½", you have passed the test! Repeat the test as needed to make sure you can confidently sew a perfect ¼" seam.

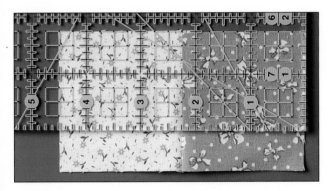

Sewing Comfortably

Other elements that promote pleasant sewing are good lighting, a comfortable chair, background music—and chocolate! Good lighting promotes accurate sewing. The better you can see what you are working on, the better your results. A comfortable chair enables you to sew for longer periods of time. An office chair with a good back rest and adjustable height works well. Music helps keep you relaxed. Chocolate is, for many quilters, simply a necessity.

Tips for Patchwork and Pressing

As you sew more patchwork, you'll develop your own shortcuts and favorite methods. Here are a few favored by many quilters:

- As you join patchwork units to form rows, and join rows to form blocks, press seams in opposite directions from row to row whenever possible (*Photo A*). By pressing seams one direction in the first row and the opposite direction in the next row, you will often create seam allowances that abut when rows are joined (*Photo B*). Abutting or nesting seams are ideal for forming perfectly matched corners on the right side of your quilt blocks and quilt top. Such pressing is not always possible, so don't worry if you end up with seam allowances facing the same direction as you join units.

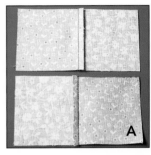 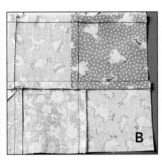

- Sew on and off a small, folded fabric square to prevent bobbin thread from bunching at throat plate (*Photo C*). You'll also save thread, which means fewer stops to wind bobbins, and fewer hanging threads to be snipped. Repeated use of the small piece of fabric gives it lots of thread "legs," so some quilters call it a spider.

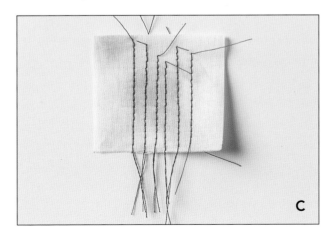

● Chain piece patchwork to reduce the amount of thread you use, and minimize the number and length of threads you need to trim from patchwork. Without cutting threads at the end of a seam, take 3–4 stitches without any fabric under the needle, creating a short thread chain approximately ⅛" long (*Photo D*). Repeat until you have a long line of pieces. Remove chain from machine, clip threads between units, and press seams.

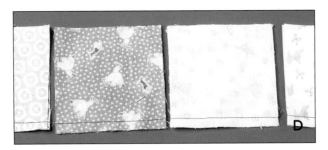

● Trim off tiny triangle tips (sometimes called dog ears) created when making triangle-square units (*Photo E*). Trimming triangles reduces bulk and makes patchwork units and blocks lie flatter. Though no one will see the back of your quilt top once it's quilted, a neat back free of dangling threads and patchwork points is the mark of a good quilter. Also, a smooth, flat quilt top is easier to quilt, whether by hand or machine.

● Careful pressing will make your patchwork neat and crisp, and will help make your finished quilt top lie flat. Ironing and pressing are two different skills. Iron fabric to remove wrinkles using a back and forth, smoothing motion. Press patchwork and quilt blocks by raising and gently lowering the iron atop your work. After sewing a patchwork unit, first press the seam with the unit closed, pressing to set, or embed, the stitching. Setting the seam this way will help produce straight, crisp seams. Open the unit and press on the right side with the seam toward the darkest

fabric, being careful to not form a pleat in your seam, and carefully pressing the patchwork flat.

● Many quilters use finger pressing to open and flatten seams of small units before pressing with an iron. To finger press, open patchwork unit with right side of fabric facing you. Run your fingernail firmly along seam, making sure unit is fully open with no pleat.

● Careful use of steam in your iron will make seams and blocks crisp and flat (*Photo F*). Aggressive ironing can stretch blocks out of shape, and is a common pitfall for new quilters.

Adding Borders

Follow these simple instructions to make borders that fit perfectly on your quilt.

1. Find the length of your quilt by measuring through the quilt center, not along the edges, since the edges may have stretched. Take 3 measurements and average them to determine the length to cut your side borders (*Diagram A*). Cut 2 side borders this length.

2. Fold border strips in half to find center. Pinch to create crease mark or place a pin at center. Fold quilt top in half crosswise to find center of side. Attach side borders to quilt center by pinning them at the ends and the center, and easing in any fullness. If quilt edge is a bit longer than border, pin and sew with border on top; if border is

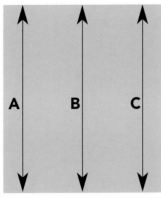

Diagram A

A _____

B _____

C _____

TOTAL _____

_____ ÷3

AVERAGE
LENGTH _____

HELPFUL TIP
**Use the following decimal conversions to calculate
your quilt's measurements:**

⅛" = .125	⅝" = .625
¼" = .25	¾" = .75
⅜" = .375	⅞" = .875
½" = .5	

slightly longer than quilt top, pin and sew with border on the bottom. Machine feed dogs will ease in the fullness of the longer piece. Press seams toward borders.

3. Find the width of your quilt by measuring across the quilt and side borders (*Diagram B*). Take 3 measurements and average them to determine the length to cut your top and bottom borders. Cut 2 borders this length.

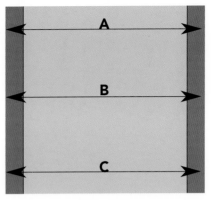

Diagram B

4. Mark centers of borders and top and bottom edges of quilt top. Attach top and bottom borders to quilt, pinnning at ends and center, and easing in any fullness (*Diagram C*). Press seams toward borders.

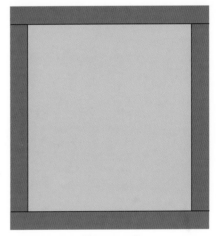

Diagram C

5. Gently steam press entire quilt top on one side and then the other. When pressing on wrong side, trim off any loose threads.

Joining Border Strips

Not all quilts have borders, but they are a nice complement to a quilt top. If your border is longer than 40", you will need to join 2 or more strips to make a border the required length. You can join border strips with either a straight seam parallel to the ends of the strips (*Photo A* on page 138), or with a diagonal seam. For the diagonal seam method, place one border strip perpendicular to another strip, rights sides facing (*Photo B*). Stitch diagonally across strips as shown. Trim seam allowance to ¼". Press seam open (*Photo C*).

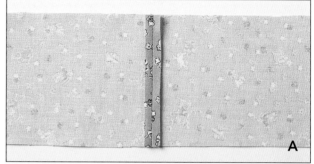

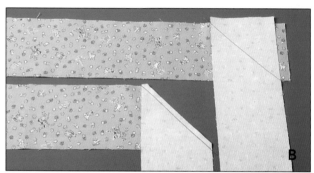

Quilting Your Quilt

Quilters today joke that there are three ways to quilt a quilt—by hand, by machine, or by check. Some enjoy making quilt tops so much, they prefer to hire a professional machine quilter to finish their work. The Split Nine Patch baby quilt shown at left has simple machine quilting that you can do yourself.

Decide what color thread will look best on your quilt top before choosing your backing fabric. A thread color that will blend in with the quilt top is a good choice for beginners. Choose backing fabric that will blend with your thread as well. A print fabric is a good choice for hiding less-than-perfect machine quilting. The backing fabric must be at least 3"–4" larger than your quilt top on all 4 sides. For example: if your quilt top measures 44" × 44", your backing needs to be at least 50" × 50". If your quilt top is 80" × 96", then your backing fabric needs to be at least 86" × 102".

For quilt tops 36" wide or less, use a single width of fabric for the backing. Buy enough length to allow adequate margin at quilt edges, as noted above. When your quilt is wider than 36", one option is to use 60"-, 90"-, or 108"-wide fabric for the quilt backing. Because fabric selection is limited for wide fabrics, quilters generally piece the quilt backing from 44/45"-wide fabric. Plan on 40"–42" of usable fabric width when estimating how much fabric to purchase. Plan your piecing strategy to avoid having a seam along the vertical or horizontal center of the quilt.

For a quilt 37"–60" wide, a backing with horizontal seams is usually the most economical use of fabric. For example, for a quilt 50" × 70", vertical seams would require 152", or 4¼ yards, of 44/45"-wide fabric (76" + 76" = 152"). Horizontal seams would require 112", or 3¼ yards (56" + 56" = 112").

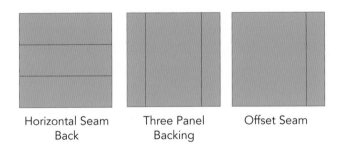

Horizontal Seam Back   Three Panel Backing   Offset Seam

For a quilt 61"–80" wide, most quilters piece a three-panel backing, with vertical seams, from two lengths of fabric. Cut one of the pieces in half lengthwise, and sew the halves to opposite sides of the wider panel. Press the seams away from the center panel.

For a quilt 81"–120" wide, you will need three lengths of fabric, plus extra margin. For example, for a quilt 108" × 108", purchase at least 342", or 9½ yards, of 44/45"-wide fabric (114" + 114" + 114" = 342").

For a three-panel backing, pin the selvage edge of the center panel to the selvage edge of the side panel, with edges aligned and right sides facing. Machine stitch with a ½" seam. Trim seam allowances to ¼", trimming off the selvages from both panels at once. Press the seam away from the center of the quilt. Repeat on other side of center panel.

For a two-panel backing, join panels in the same manner as above, and press the seam to one side.

Create a "quilt sandwich" by layering your backing, batting, and quilt top. Find the crosswise center of the backing fabric by folding it in half. Mark with a pin on each side. Lay backing down on a table or floor, wrong side up. Tape corners and edges of backing to the surface with masking or painter's tape so that backing is taut (*Photo A*).

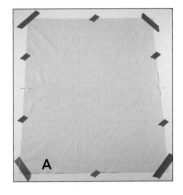

Fold batting in half crosswise and position it atop backing fabric, centering folded edge at center of backing (*Photo B*). Unfold batting and smooth it out atop backing (*Photo C*).

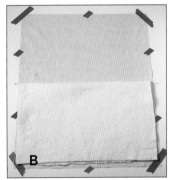
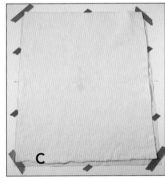

In the same manner, fold the quilt top in half crosswise and center it atop backing and batting (*Photo D*). Unfold top and smooth it out atop batting (*Photo E*).

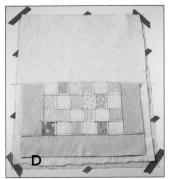

Use safety pins to pin baste the layers (*Photo F*). Pins should be about a fist width apart. A special tool, called a Kwik Klip, or a grapefruit spoon makes closing the pins easier. As you slide a pin through all three layers, slide the point of the pin into one of the tool's grooves. Push on the tool to help close the pin.

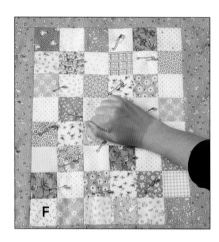

For straight line quilting, install an even feed or walking foot on your machine. This presser foot helps all three layers of your quilt move through the machine evenly without bunching.

Walking Foot

Stitching "in the ditch"

An easy way to quilt your first quilt is to stitch "in the ditch" along seam lines. No marking is needed for this type of quilting.

Binding Your Quilt

Preparing Binding

Strips for quilt binding may be cut either on the straight of grain or on the bias.

1. Measure the perimeter of your quilt and add approximately 24" to allow for mitered corners and finished ends.
2. Cut the number of strips necessary to achieve desired length. We like to cut binding strips 2¼" wide.
3. Join your strips with diagonal seams into 1 continuous piece (*Photo A*). Press the seams open. (See page 137 for instructions for the diagonal seams method of joining strips.)

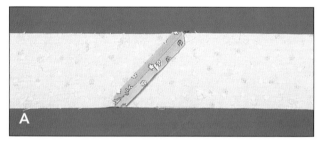

4. Press your binding in half lengthwise, with wrong sides facing, to make French-fold binding (*Photo B*).

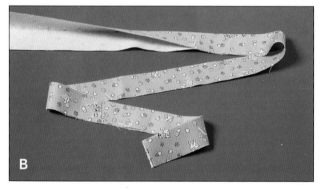

Attaching Binding

Attach the binding to your quilt using an even-feed or walking foot. This prevents puckering when sewing through the three layers.

1. Choose beginning point along one side of quilt. Do not start at a corner. Match the two raw edges of the binding strip to the raw edge of the quilt top. The folded edge

will be free and to left of seam line (*Photo C*). Leave 12" or longer tail of binding strip dangling free from beginning point. Stitch, using ¼" seam, through all layers.

2. For mitered corners, stop stitching ¼" from corner; backstitch, and remove quilt from sewing machine (*Photo D*). Place a pin ¼" from corner to mark where you will stop stitching.

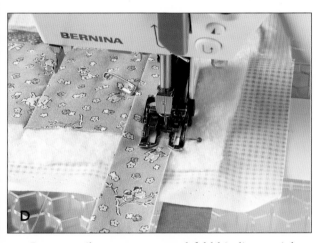

Rotate quilt quarter turn and fold binding straight up, away from corner, forming 45-degree-angle fold (*Photo E*).

Bring binding straight down in line with next edge to be sewn, leaving top fold even with raw edge of previously sewn side (*Photo F*). Begin stitching at top edge, sewing through all layers (*Photo G*).

3. To finish binding, stop stitching about 8" away from starting point, leaving about a 12" tail at end (*Photo H*). Bring beginning and end of binding to center of 8" opening and fold each back, leaving about ¼" space

between the two folds of binding (*Photo I*). (Allowing this ¼" extra space is critical, as binding tends to stretch when it is stitched to the quilt. If the folded ends meet at this point, your binding will be too long for the space after the ends are joined.) Crease folds of binding with your fingernail.

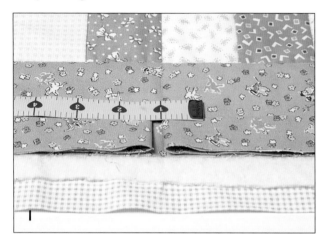

4. Open out each edge of binding and draw line across wrong side of binding on creased fold line, as shown in *Photo J*. Draw line along lengthwise fold of binding at same spot to create an X (*Photo K*).

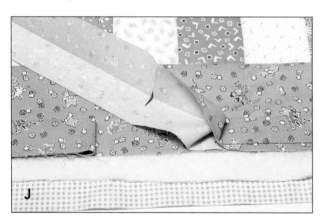

5. With edge of ruler at marked X, line up 45-degree-angle marking on ruler with one long side of binding (*Photo L*). Draw diagonal line across binding as shown in *Photo M*.

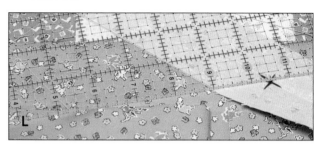

Repeat for other end of binding. Lines must angle in same direction (*Photo N*).

6. Pin binding ends together with right sides facing, pin-matching diagonal lines as shown in *Photo O*. Binding ends will be at right angles to each other. Machine-stitch along diagonal line, removing pins as you stitch (*Photo P*).

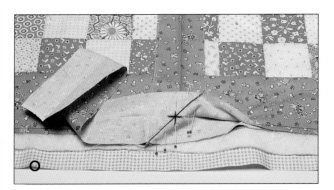

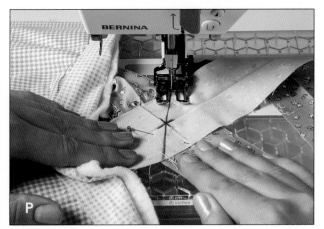

7. Lay binding against quilt to double-check that it is correct length (*Photo Q*). Trim ends of binding ¼" from diagonal seam (*Photo R*).

8. Finger press diagonal seam open (*Photo S*). Fold binding in half and finish stitching binding to quilt (*Photo T*).

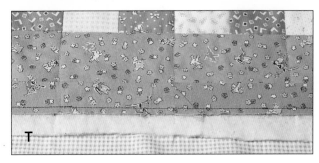

Hand Stitching Binding to Quilt Back

1. Trim any excess batting and quilt back with scissors or a rotary cutter (*Photo A*). Leave enough batting (about ⅛" beyond quilt top) to fill binding uniformly when it is turned to quilt back.

2. Bring folded edge of binding to quilt back so that it covers machine stitching. Blindstitch folded edge to quilt backing, using a few pins just ahead of stitching to hold binding in place (*Photo B*).

3. Continue stitching to corner. Fold unstitched binding from next side under, forming a 45-degree angle and a mitered corner. Stitch mitered folds on both front and back (*Photo C*).

Finishing Touches

● **Label your quilt so the recipient and future generations know who made it.** To make a label, use a fabric marking pen to write the details on a small piece of solid color fabric (*Photo A*). To make writing easier, put pieces of masking tape on the wrong side. Remove tape after writing. Use your iron to turn under ¼" on each edge, then stitch the label to the back of your quilt using a blindstitch, taking care not to sew through to quilt top.

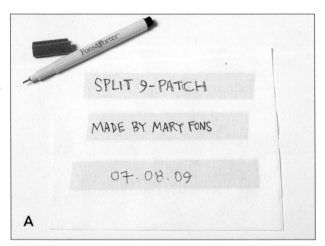

● **Take a photo of your quilt.** Keep your photos in an album or journal along with notes, fabric swatches, and other information about the quilts.

● **If your quilt is a gift, include care instructions.** Some quilt shops carry pre-printed care labels you can sew onto the quilt (*Photo B*). Or, make a care label using the method described above.

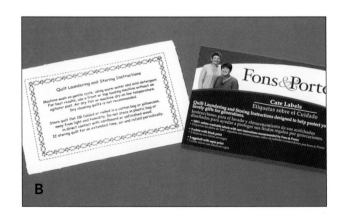